Get Married Now

To Alan,

With Best

Regards,

Get Married Now

The Definitive Guide for Finding & Marrying The Right Mate for You

Hilary Rich

BOB ADAMS, INC.
PUBLISHERS
Holbrook, Massachusetts

Published by Bob Adams, Inc.
260 Center Street, Holbrook, MA 02343

ISBN: 1-55850-243-2

Printed in the United States of America.

J   I   H   G   F   E   D   C   B   A

This book is available at quantity discounts for bulk purchases. For information, call 1-800-872-5627.

This publication is designed to provide accurate and authoritative information with regard to the subject matter covered. It is sold with the understanding that the publisher is not engaged in rendering legal, accounting, or other professional advice. If legal advice or other expert assistance is required, the services of a competent professional person should be sought.
— From a *Declaration of Principles* jointly adopted by a Committee of the American Bar Association and a Committee of Publishers and Associations

COVER DESIGN: Marshall Henrichs.

Dedication

To my best friend,
my husband, Steven

Acknowledgments

The following people have had a great impact on my life and I would like to acknowledge them. They are what made it possible for me to write this book.

To Steven, my husband, who loves me for who I am, and supports me toward who I want to become. He believed in me and took care of the outside distractions and pressures so I could write this book.

To Cynthia Citron, my mother, who gives me an unlimited supply of love and support, and whose radiant sense of humor taught me that life is to be enjoyed.

To Robert Citron, my father, who taught me that you can accomplish anything you dream of with enthusiasm and persistence.

To Frank and Gertrude Citron, my grandparents, whose love, guidance, and example taught me to appreciate the value of family.

To Eva and Harvey Rich, my in-laws, who taught me the true meaning of the word "mensch", how to give of yourself for another.

To Kirk Citron, Gavriella Aber, and Dena Samuels, my siblings, who are always there for me, and whose love and friendship is so precious to me. And special appreciation to Dena for her insights and encouragement in writing this book.

To Eileen Lizer, who introduced me to my husband, and to whom I owe the rest of my entire life.

To Peter Stolz, my cousin, who started me on the journey of taking control of my own life, and whose wisdom I've come to depend on.

To my Rabbi, who taught me about character and truth, and

who is a constant source of inspiration to me.

To Jerome Downes, my teacher, who trained me in what it means to be committed, and for challenging me to create my own future.

To Alyss Dorese, my literary agent, whose insight, guidance and wit made the publishing process a growing experience and a joy.

To Brandon Toropov and Lisa Fisher at Bob Adams, Inc., whose enthusiasm and expertise were invaluable to me.

Table of Contents

Foreword

The first time I met Hilary, she told me that she was getting married the next summer. I didn't know her, but I congratulated her warmly and inquired about the groom. She said she hadn't met him yet, and in fact had no one particular in mind.

She then proceeded to tell me all about him. She described his character traits, his values, and what was important to him. I was so moved by how she talked about this man that I reached out and squeezed her hand. When she finished, I said, "I know the man that you've just described!" I stood up, went over to the phone and dialed the number of a man I knew who seemed to match her description. They went out the following weekend.

At their wedding that summer, I learned from Hilary's family and friends that I was one of the stones she had resolutely refused to leave unturned. She had made the commitment to get married, and had designed a plan of action to accomplish her mission. Here, in this book, you will find that plan.

To all of you who follow this plan, I congratulate you warmly.

— *Eileen Lizer*

Read This First

THERE ARE MILLIONS of people in this country who want to get married. The trend is away from the casual attitude regarding relationships toward more traditional values of home and family. In short, the sexual revolution is over, and AIDS has everyone searching for a monogamous relationship.

Those on the career track are ready to share their lives with someone. Sworn bachelors are now recognizing their need for the comforts of marriage. "Biological clocks" are ticking. Widows and divorcees are looking to build new relationships on more stable ground. And the culture around us is changing, as well. Businesses that cater to singles are booming. Newspapers are filled with personal ads, and singles events draw record crowds.

So why is it so difficult to find a mate? Is it because people are too busy? Because they don't make marriage a priority in their lives? Because they are afraid to make the commitment? Because they are resigned to the idea that "it won't work out"? My guess is that much of the problem lies in an uncertainty about what to do. Perhaps if more people knew about the *how* of finding and marrying the best mate, and acted on this knowledge, they could get married in spite of all the other challenges.

The book you are holding gives you step-by-step instructions on exactly *how* to find and marry the best mate for you. It tells you what you should look for, and how you will know when you've found the right person. It covers the emotional and environmental obstacles that may be standing in your way. It tells you about the best places to find your mate and shows you how to prepare yourself for marriage. It explains how to manage the important project of finding a mate, and how to keep yourself motivated and committed from beginning to end. *Get Married Now* also explains how to develop a stable relationship so that your marriage will last a lifetime.

This book also empowers you to act on the knowledge you obtain. Instead of just suggesting an idea, I have tried to make the book as practical as possible by explaining exactly how to accomplish each step of the process. Taking a project and making it into a list of smaller items to do makes it much easier to accomplish each objective. I have done my best to make the process so clear and straightforward that even someone who is sidetracked easily (like me) could stay motivated through all of it!

This will be a big project for you. I guess if I told you that it was going to be easy, I might make you feel better, but we'd both know it wasn't true. One thing is for sure, though: If you keep doing what you've always done, it will likely get you what you've already got! If you follow the steps in this book from point A to point Z, odds are that you'll end up where you want to be—on the altar. That's a lot better than wishing and hoping for offers.

You can at least take heart in the fact that you won't have to re-invent the wheel—like I did! I sat around for five years waiting for "Mr. Right" to show up. Oh, I dated plenty. I even found some men who were completely wrong for me and tried to convince myself that they were right. I commiserated with my girlfriends; I read horrifying statistics comparing my chances of getting married to those of my being struck by lightning; but mostly I just felt sorry for myself.

Then one day I told myself that I was not going to wait any longer. I had a lot to offer a future mate, and I realized that if I wanted to get married, *I* was going to have to make it happen. I knew that I had to make this a major project in my life—or I might have to wait for another five years or even longer.

I realized that most of us grew up assuming we would get married, but that no one ever told us how. So I searched bookstores, the library, and magazine articles for information on the subject. I talked to a lot of people who had advice for me. But I was not thrilled with the results—and I was not willing to waste any more time. I couldn't seem to find what I was looking for: a strategy for the best and most efficient way to find my future husband.

I had to take everything that I had learned and create my own system. I ran into many obstacles, and I had to invent ways around them. But the bottom line is that after seven months of implementing my plan, I met the most wonderful human being on the face of this earth, my husband Steven.

So—this book will lay out the guidelines for you. The system you will read about has worked not only for me, but also for many, many participants in my *Get Married Now* seminars. Even if you have tried everything and given up hope, this book will give you a powerful new perspective on finding your mate. It will help you to overcome the fear of marrying the wrong person, because you will have a clear picture of what you need and how to find it.

With the staggering divorce rates, you need to be as careful about your selection as possible. Brenda, a seminar participant, told me that my system gave her the hands-on tools she needed to maintain and strengthen her motivation and discernment for finding the right mate. She told me that the ideas you are about to encounter may well have saved her and others from years of heartache and disappointment. After working this plan, she met and married John, and I was fortunate enough to be invited to attend their beautiful wedding. It was a magnificent ceremony held in front of a quiet pond—with swans, flowers, and hundreds of guests.

This book is a road leading to exactly where you want to go. All you have to do is put one foot in front of the other and walk, step by step. I have tried to provide a great deal of support along the way, but if you prefer to work with a friend you feel comfortable with, you will find that this book also works very well with partners. The best way to work together is to read each chapter and then review your notebook section answers together. If the going gets rough, just remember that all each of you needs to do is to find *one* person!

There are many stories included here from the three years I have been coaching people about getting married. All of the names and details have been altered to preserve the anonymity of those who so generously shared their stories with me. I would greatly appreciate hearing your comments and success stories, too. I save all of these letters, and who knows—maybe one day I'll turn them into another book! You can write to me in care of the publisher, Bob Adams, Inc. at 260 Center Street, Holbrook, Massachusetts, 02343.

I hope that this book will help you to find and marry the most wonderful, loving person in the world for you. I know what it's like to sit around wishing and hoping. Here is your big chance to make your dream a reality, to take the future into your own hands. I wish you a life filled with joy and happiness. May you share it with someone very special.

— Hilary Rich

1

Emotional Preparation

YOU WANT TO GET MARRIED. Maybe you have wanted to for a long time. Maybe you have tried everything and nothing has worked. So: what's going to be different this time?

This time, you will know exactly what to do and how to do it. Sounds easy enough; but what if it gets difficult and you want to give up? What is it going to take to *make it* work this time? Well, I'll tell you.

The fundamental step of emotional preparation for marriage is to *make the commitment to get married*. I know this sounds simplistic, but I can't tell you the number of people I talk to who are indecisive about this issue. They *say* that they want to get married . . . then they say that maybe they aren't ready, that they would be ready if they met the right person, that they don't want to get married until they resolve their career situation—there are dozens of excuses. No wonder these people aren't progressing! One foot's in, one foot's out. Where are you?

In order to maximize your power over your own future, you need to make the commitment to get married and stick to that commitment through thick, through thin, through times when you don't feel like it, and through anything else until you are happily married. Making this commitment to yourself might be difficult, but it is truly the ideal practice for making the commitment of marriage to someone for the rest of your life.

The problem is that the very word "commitment" is enough to make some people want to crawl under a rock. It conjures up images of all the past commitments they've made to themselves or to others that they have gloriously broken. Feelings of guilt and burden are often associated with this word, which is unfortunate because, if you look back through history, the great individuals who have really made a difference in the world are those who have made strong commitments. Yet, there remains this fear of commitment because when you look at your own life, the myriad of broken commitments follow you around like a ball and chain. How many diets have you broken? How many workout schedules have you given up on? In fact, how many times have you made the commitment to get married only to get resigned and give up? Well if this book does nothing else but assist you to *get* committed and *stay* committed to getting married, it will have been well worth your investment.

But before we begin that process, there is something very important that you must do. You must forgive yourself for all of the past things that you committed to but didn't do. When I was making my commitment to getting married, the biggest obstacle standing in my way was the fact that I had made so many other promises that I hadn't kept. My exercise routine consisted of hitting the snooze button just enough times so that there would be no time left for me to go running in the morning. My weekly letters to my sister were now going out on a monthly basis, and I had broken two appointments in the past week because of a conflicting schedule. In other words, I couldn't see how someone as unreliable as I was could make such a huge commitment as getting married, and to select a date by when I intended to get married! This is when I recognized that a lot of other people also have a hard time keeping commitments. When I took a look at the successful people that I admired, what I noticed was that they seemed to have a better track record of keeping commitments than I did because (and here's the key difference) they still kept making commitments even when they didn't keep old ones. With this goal in mind, I decided to forgive myself for all of my past broken commitments, and, with total determination, I made the commitment to get married. If you want to do yourself a favor, forgive yourself for all of your past broken commitments and get back in the game of making commitments. It's time to make the awesome commitment of getting married.

Step One: Commit!
The first step is to make your commitment as specific as possible. Examples: I will be married by December 31. I will meet the woman of my dreams by June 15, and will be engaged by November 15.

Write this down in your notebook at the end of this chapter now, before you go on to step two. This process psychologically changes your thinking from "someday my prince will come," to putting everything into real terms. This date will become emblazoned in your mind and motivate you to give it all you've got! And be sure to put the date far enough into the future so that it is possible.

This can be confronting, but it also puts a level of ease into your search. You know that if this person isn't the right one, the next one will be in order to achieve your "by when" date. A woman I spoke to named Cheryl said that as soon as she made the commitment to get engaged by December 31, she no longer spent so much time trying to impress every man she met. She suddenly had the confidence to just be herself, secure that she would accomplish her mission by her date.

Don't take my word for it! Try it and you will see how your mind relaxes. The reality of the date gives you renewed determination to pursue your vision of being married to the perfect mate! If the date that you selected passes and you're not married, pick another date right away. This is psychologically very important. (Make sure you don't keep this option of picking another date as a "back door" to firmly committing to the first date you selected.)

Step Two: Face the Obstacles

The second step is to be prepared for the obstacles that will get in your way. They hit you in the face the second after you make a huge commitment, and you see just how far you have to go to accomplish your mission! Before I had made the commitment to get married, I used to wake up in the morning thinking about the day's activities. But afterward, what occupied my mind is just how unmarried I was, and just how much I had to do to get what I wanted. I felt sorry for myself, and the fact that I didn't have a "significant other" to commiserate with made me feel even worse. There were times when I filled my schedule to capacity in order to distract myself from facing the facts. But what helped me a lot was recognizing that, in order to get where I wanted to be, I was going to have to face the obstacles in my way. In my case it was my tendency to fill an emotional void with activities that helped me avoid my situation. I worked hard to overcome this by focusing my energies on getting married.

Making a commitment puts an issue at the forefront of your mind, which is valuable in getting it accomplished. However, in the case of getting married, it can also be sad. When you are caught up in the business of life, it is easy to push your desire to be married to the back of your mind, where it doesn't bother you. Try your best to see what your own obstacles are, and do your best to think of ways to overcome them.

Some people find that committing to getting married occupies all of their immediate thoughts. Their present situations are hard to face day in and day out. Some people remain unmarried for years because they would rather keep busy and occupied than face reality. It will take a lot of strength for you to face this on a daily basis until you are married. A way to make it bearable is to have friends that you can confide in. Verbalize how difficult and sad it is. You can find a good therapist to talk to and support you through your search. Or you can get busy with your action plan to find a spouse—at least you will be moving constantly toward your goal! Also, just keep saying to yourself, "This is it. I am getting married by such and such date, and nothing is going to stand in my way—not sadness, not resignation, not rejection, and not anybody!"

Step Three: Create a Support System

The third step is to surround yourself with people who support your commitment, not with people who have given up hope, are resigned to the single life, and try to knock down your commitment. Find friends or family members who will support you at eleven o'clock at night, and who will listen to your stories about this horrible date you just had! You need people who will be there when the going gets rough. They are very difficult to find, but it's better to have nobody than a saboteur who would hate to see you succeed at getting married.

A man named Carl who wanted to get married lived with two other bachelors who were "partying types." In relating the story to me, he said that every time he started to get serious with someone, his roommates would take him out on the town and convince him that she wasn't the right one for him. At first, he respected their opinions, so he would call the relationship off. But after it happened too many times, he got wise and stopped listening to them.

In that environment, Carl didn't stand a chance. It's even better to talk to a dog or stuffed animal rather than someone who is going to be destructive of your mission! By choosing your friends carefully and following the information in Chapter 2 on environmental preparation you will be setting yourself up to succeed.

Looking at the Obstacles

This section on making the commitment to getting married is probably the most important part of this book. Refer back to it often, especially during difficult times. Staying committed is what separates the single people from people who are married. Don't you want to be in the latter category? Following are some of the major obstacles that may stand in the way of your commitment, and of your getting married. Some of the issues raised will take more than one reading to understand thoroughly. Working them through will not only make your job of finding someone more successful, but you will be happier when you get there.

Haunted by the Past

Overcoming the past may be difficult, but it is vital to the future success of your relationships. As much as people feel that they are self-made people in charge of their own destinies, at a certain point we must acknowledge (at least to ourselves!) that we are a product of our histories. Our pasts weave their way through our lives affecting our interactions and relationships with people in ways that we may not even see. There may be unresolved issues from our childhoods that prevent us from getting what we really want out of life. Examples might be feelings of anger toward parents, feelings of competitiveness with siblings, or feelings of neglect and abuse.

Brenda wanted desperately to get married. She had been in a series of relationships that she considered healthy. It wasn't until closer examination that she realized that all of them had been long-distance relationships. This seemed very curious to her. In speaking with a therapist, she discovered that since her father had moved across the country after divorcing her mother, she had developed a pattern of loving men "long distance." She could see how each of her relationships had modeled itself after her primary relationship with her father. This valuable insight helped her to work toward a more stable relationship with a man that lived nearby.

Just getting over your parents' divorce or bad marriage, or your own past relationships, can take a lot of time and effort. One reason people don't tackle these issues is their fear of failure, or because they feel as if burying the feelings under a rug will get the feelings out of the way. The only problem is they keep tripping over their buried emotions, and sooner or later these issues must be resolved.

The process of uncovering these issues, which may be subconscious, and working them through can be difficult, and many people seek the advice of trained therapists. This not only makes the process easier, but also makes sure once and for all that all the obstacles are out of the way to finding a truly satisfying relationship. Many people, however, find this solution to be unthinkable, as if something were wrong with them. But, in reality, the healthiest people are the ones who are always trying to be the best that they can be, and if that means admitting they are not perfect, they are willing to do so. But this is a decision that each person must make for him- or herself.

There are other ways to overcome unresolved issues from the past. They include reading self-help books, joining various self-help groups that are geared toward your particular issues, and even having long conversations with your parents or siblings that raise these issues in a constructive manner. My friend Beth had always been resentful that her father seemed to care more about watching football than he did about her. She finally got up the courage and told him that this had always bothered her, and that all she wanted was to be closer to him. She was surprised at his reaction. He was shocked that it bothered her. He said that when she had been a teenager, she seemed to not want to have anything to do with him, and he always felt like he was butting into her life. They talked for a very long time, and the end result is that they are much closer now, and that she has gained the powerful ability to communicate her feelings better. This is invaluable for her future relationships!

Old harbored feelings must be released, old wounds healed, and everything forgiven. This can be difficult to do. Having a good friend to practice this conversation with can be a good way to gear up for this. It is important to start out these types of conversations by saying that you are not trying to dump angry feelings on everyone, you just need to get some things off your chest so that you can develop a better relationship. Your intent is not to hurt your loved ones, rather to get closer to them, so be very careful with everything you say. It may take many such conversations till you get out what you really want to say.

Most people think that burying old wounds will make them go away, but we all know from experience that they just seem to fester and become even more destructive in our lives. It takes strong motivation to deal with these issues once and for all. It is a very important step in your emotional preparation for getting married. Until you have the old issues resolved, "Mr. or Ms. Magic" is not going to come along and be so perfect that all of your emotional baggage will mysteriously disappear! In fact the opposite is true, your baggage will weigh down your future relationship. You don't want to drag all your old issues with you into a bright new relationship! If you work these issues through, what is possible in a new relationship is a comfort, closeness, and stability you never thought possible.

Staying Stuck

The tendency for people to stay in bad relationships is also a serious issue that gets in the way of getting married. They are so happy to have someone around that they stay in these relationships for years sometimes, just to avoid being alone. They are neither satisfied nor fulfilled, and with every passing year they get farther and farther from what they truly want out of life. What exacerbates this problem is that they keep talking themselves into staying in the relationship or hoping that one day "he'll change," or "she'll change."

At the heart of this issue is addiction—people are actually addicted to these dysfunctional relationships. They have a history, often since childhood, of unhealthy relationships. They repeat these patterns over and over again. And when they meet someone who fits into this dysfunctional pattern, they are duped into thinking that since it feels familiar, it must be "right." This could be where the term "chemistry" came from: instant attraction, without thought about whether this person is right or not.

Very often people do not feel comfortable in stable, healthy relationships because they just aren't used to them. This is very sad, but unfortunately extremely common. One thirty-eight-year-old woman named Janet said that she would like to get married, but that her current boyfriend just wasn't ready to make that commitment. He did not feel that he could commit to marriage when he wasn't financially stable. Janet had been with him for three years, and his career wasn't any more stable now than it had been three years earlier.

It turns out that Janet had come from a family whose future financial security was always in question. Thus, she felt "comfortable" in her relationship because it paralleled her childhood patterns. Of course it wasn't healthy for her, nor was she getting what she truly wanted out of life, but the patterns were so strong that breaking out of them would take an enormous amount of effort. I am not sure what Janet ended up doing, probably staying in that relationship and wishing her life would turn out better (as if some outside force had control of her life), rather than taking control of it herself. But it is really too bad. If she could only see how her childhood patterns are keeping her from a healthy, stable, secure relationship, maybe she would be motivated to either change this relationship or find someone new who didn't fit these patterns.

It is very important to start examining the factors that make a healthy and stable relationship, and begin the process of breaking from your current patterns of behavior. Again, many people have a much easier time breaking these patterns with the help of a therapist. Whatever works is fine, but if you are one of those people who is clinging to a relationship that is not leading toward marriage, or repeats all the dysfunctional patterns you have come to be familiar with, it is time to do some work to break free of these patterns. It is time to get on with what you truly want to have out of life. The elusive dream of "someday everything will turn out just the way I want it to" begins with a single step from you, and is followed by dedicated action, day after day, until you have succeeded in getting what you want.

Lack of Role Models

Many people grew up without any role models of stable, healthy relationships. This makes it very difficult for them to create stable, healthy relationships for themselves. The only picture they have in their minds is of the "Hollywood" couples that they see in the movies that are always happy and "perfect." This fantasy is what they are looking for in their mates, and that is why they are never happy or satisfied with their relationships. These types may be thrilling for a few weeks or months, but they will never meet your expectations or needs over the long haul. Glamour is fleeting, but there is nothing that can replace the nurturing effects of having someone care for you day in and day out for years and years. The only way you are ever going to find a "real" person is to give up your search for the Hollywood fantasy, and start examining what you really *need* to make you happy. A gorgeous, sexy Romeo might sweep you off your feet, but when you're married with two kids in diapers, who else is he out sweeping off her feet?

This is the time for you to be pragmatic and to throw romantic ideas out the window. Because people lack role models, they don't have any idea what it takes to have stable, healthy relationships, and not only do they look for the wrong things in their mates, when they find the perfect candidates, they don't even recognize them!

I spoke to Jeff at a dinner party and he told me that he had a very clear picture of what he was looking for in a mate. She had to be very beautiful, kind, loving, and adventuresome. He had been dating a woman for two months, but at the same time continued to go on many other dates. When I asked him about this one woman, he told me that she was very kind, was very close to her family, and seemed to have good values. He said that he really enjoyed being with her, but that she just didn't excite him. Maybe it was that she was too plain in looks and in personality. He really wanted to marry someone that scuba dived or jumped out of airplanes. When I asked him why, he said because he liked excitement. But if you think about it, Jeff may find a beautiful, exciting woman, and they may have a terrible, dysfunctional relationship. This woman he is dating might have all of the qualities that would make Jeff the happiest husband in the world, but he will miss them because of his fantasy "pictures" of what he wants.

Many people do not know what is best for them, or what would make them extraordinarily happy. In the section on making a list in Chapter 3, you are going to be quite surprised that almost every solitary personal ad advertises the exact things that are least important to a successful relationship. In that chapter, you will start to see the kinds of things to look for that *will* make you happy. For now, start picking apart your own Hollywood image of "Mr. or Ms. Right," and start looking for role models of healthy, stable relationships.

NOTEBOOK

1. List ten commitments that you have broken in the past year.

1. _____

2. _____

3. _____

4. _____

5. _____

6. _____

7. _____

8. _____

9. _____

10. _____

2. How does this make you feel about yourself, and about your ability to keep commitments?

_____

_____

_____

3. Are you willing to forgive yourself for these past broken commitments?

_____

_____

_____

4. Is your determination to get married big enough for you to make the commitment to get married?

_____

_____

_____

5. The first step is to make your commitment as specific as possible. Write your commitment here, and also put it on a note to put on your bathroom mirror! (Examples: I will be married by December 31. I will be engaged by November 15.)

_____

_____

_____

_____

6. The second step is to be prepared for the obstacles that will get in your way. Make a list of these obstacles. (Examples: I will get rejected and give up. My Mom will bug me. I will find other more pressing issues to occupy my time.)

_____

_____

_____

_____

7. The third step is to create a support system around you that supports your commitment. What specific actions will you take to accomplish this? (Examples: I will call a friend and tell them about this project.)

_____

_____

_____

_____

8. What problems have you had in relationships that you keep having over and over again?

_____

_____

_____

_____

9. What issues do you wish were resolved and complete in your relationships with people?

_____

_____

_____

_____

10. What aspects of your childhood are you angry about that may interfere with your current relationships?

_____

_____

_____

11. What emotional baggage do you carry around with you that you would like to get rid of?

_____

_____

_____

_____

12. What actions will you take to resolve these issues? (Examples: Read books. Talk to a therapist. Talk with my family.)

_____

_____

_____

13. Why have you stayed in unhealthy relationships?

_____

_____

_____

14. What kind of support structure could you build to help you get out of these types of relationships?

_____

_____

_____

_____

15. In the left column, make a list of "Mr. or Ms. Hollywood" characteristics, in the right column, write down why that particular characteristic may not be the best one to look for in a mate. (Example: left column: gorgeous; right column: may be very self-centered.)

_____	_____
_____	_____
_____	_____
_____	_____
_____	_____
_____	_____
_____	_____
_____	_____
_____	_____
_____	_____

16. How will you begin studying healthy, stable relationships? (Examples: Read books. Talk to a therapist. Pick out role models.)

_____

_____

_____

_____

2

Environmental Preparation

AT THE SAME time that you are getting yourself emotionally prepared to get married, it is also very important that you prepare your physical environment for marriage as well. Your environment has a profound impact on your state of mind, and as a "single" person, your environment personifies those "single" qualities. It is your job to shift your environment to one that personifies the quality "marriageable."

This is *not* the time for you to start a diet or buy a new wardrobe. I can't tell you how many people keep putting this project off for yet another year with the lame excuse of wanting to lose those extra ten pounds. People will think of anything to justify putting off the scary thought of really being committed and working hard to get married. It is certainly understandable, but, remember, you want someone who will love you exactly the way you are.

As we've seen in the last chapter, trying to be Hollywood beautiful will not lead you to a strong, stable, healthy relationship. Yes you can work on your personal appearance; there's nothing wrong with trying to look attractive. In fact being neat, clean, and well groomed shows that you take pride in yourself, but this must not be your focus to find a mate. After all is said and done, you have been married for five years, and you are sitting at home watching a video together, you will only then finally believe how insignificant Hollywood characteristics are in a spouse.

Step One: Clean House
The first step in the process is to walk around your living quarters

and get rid of everything that screams out, "Single person lives here!" This might include the collection of beer bottles on your book-case, the beads from Club Med, the collection of nightclub match-books, the half burned down candles, and especially the little black book on your nightstand.

I can recall when a date came in for some tea after we had a night out together. He walked around my living room while I was in the kitchen. When I came in to sit down, he asked me what the sig-nificance was of the finished champagne bottle on the end table. Thinking fast, and not wanting to make him feel uncomfortable, I made up a story that it was from my roommate's birthday party. Not only did I feel uncomfortable about lying (and also I somehow felt that he knew I wasn't telling the truth), but it also brought back the memory of the Valentine's Day date who had given the bottle to me. This memory really did interfere with my ability to relax and enjoy the date that I was currently on. When I finally did get rid of these "single" items, it was a cathartic exercise for me. I really felt that I was readying my environment to make "Mr. Right" feel as comfortable as possible.

Step Two: Throw Away the Memories
The second step is to go through all of your old photographs of every relationship you have ever had, from the first date up until your last relationship. Gather them in one big pile, including pulling pic-tures *out* of albums. And do not let one picture slip through the cracks! Now examine these photographs very carefully. Let this be a cathartic experience, and as you look over their faces, think to your-self that all of this is behind you. You will be married soon, entering into another phase of your life. Remember the good times, and if it helps, use this review to look at some of the unresolved issues covered in the last chapter. Jot down some notes if you want to, but the main purpose of this project is to put all of your past relationships behind you.

Now it is time to get rid of every one of these pictures. This process may be very difficult to do. Even if you are in the picture and it's the best shot you've ever taken, get rid of it. If you rip the photo in half and save your side, it will always jar your memory as to whom you were standing next to at the time. Think about why you are do-ing this. When the precious person you are going to marry comes into your home, how do you think he or she will feel looking at a pic-ture of your arm around someone else? What purpose does hanging onto these photos serve? They keep you tied to the past, and it doesn't matter what anyone says, they will certainly be difficult for a future mate to live with.

My friend Amy, to whom I recommended this process, became very angry with me. How could I be so intrusive to suggest such a process? These pictures were part of her, and she felt that I wanted her to erase her past. I didn't hear from Amy for three whole weeks, and when she finally called, she was crying. She had painstakingly gone through all of her old photographs: her prom pictures, her college boyfriends, and even her old four-year relationship, and had piled them all into a box. She was calling me to help her to get up the courage to throw the box away. Amy said that she recognized how much these pictures kept her in the illusion that there were lots of men in her life. She clung to these past memories because the thought of getting rid of them made her feel too lonely. She even said she knew that hanging onto them was keeping her from making room in her life for someone else. The only advice I could think to give her was to take her time. I was encouraging of her growth process, but I also felt that she should only throw those old photos away when she was truly ready to do so.

This is your opportunity to practice taking care of another person's well-being even before you ever meet that person. Remember that your memories will not disappear. Everything valuable that you learned from these relationships will always be with you. You are just creating the space for a mate to walk through the door with nothing standing in his or her way.

This project includes mementos as well. But first, it's important to know that people who collect mementos should be admired. These people have the ability to cherish things and make ordinary things special, which is a very good quality in a mate. But, for the purpose of getting married, all of the special events and occasions having to do with past relationships only serve to interfere with your future relationship. So, for both your own clarity of the "that was then, this is now" mind-set, and the comfort of your future partner, gather up all the mementos, including old letters, keepsakes, Valentine's Day cards, pressed flowers, prom invitations, arcade stuffed animals, and even the smallest of items, and look them over before throwing them all away.

Mementos also include gifts. This is very important. If you had a relationship during which someone was materialistically generous to you, after that person is long gone, every time you wear that expensive jewelry, the cashmere sweater, the silk tie, or that perfume, you inadvertently think of that person. This subconsciously keeps you bonded to him or her in some way, and keeps you stuck in the past. You don't need to take my word for it; the second you get rid of it, you will have a sense of freedom that you haven't had in years! Just try it with even one item! Most of these items would make nice gifts for family members or friends.

You might have amassed quite a collection of gifts over the years, and some of your favorite items that you own may be from former relationships. These items are especially important to give up. However attached you are to that item is the extent to which you still cannot let go of that relationship. You've got to lay it on the line: What's more important, your future spouse, or that leather jacket?

After about a year of marriage, my husband and I were having a romantic evening at home. We had a fire burning in the fireplace, and my husband went into the kitchen to get some wine. When he returned, I was horrified at the sight of two long-stemmed glasses that a former boyfriend had given to me. I had obviously overlooked them in my "environmental preparation." My husband must have recognized the uncomfortable look on my face, because he asked me what was wrong. I told him that I had overlooked them in my "environmental cleaning," and he just laughed. Then I debated whether to drink out of the glasses or to switch them. I decided that I really didn't want to say a romantic toast with the love of my life over these old, memory-ridden glasses, so I got up and switched them.

These items really do carry the memory of the people associated with them. There is a last resort if you absolutely can't get rid of something (which I hesitate to share with you for fear that you won't get rid of everything you really should). But, for instance, if you were given a car, and cannot get rid of it for practical reasons, have a friend or family member buy the item from you for ten dollars. Have the person keep it for a week or more, and then buy it back. This way, the psychological attachment is less, and going through the process with a friend in a congenial way will create a new "history" for that article which hopefully will make it interfere less with your future relationship.

Step Three: Get Rid of Old "Dangling" Relationships

The third step is to rid yourself of old "dangling" relationships. This project may take a lot of determination, but it is incredibly powerful in preparing yourself for marriage. My friend Bill says that he dated a woman in high school who always liked him more than he liked her. In fact, when he was going off to college, she said that she would marry him in a minute if he would ever ask her. He didn't ask her then, and he never intends to ask her. But every time he breaks up a relationship, or gets rejected on too many dates, Bill calls her up and listens to her tell him how great he is. It is nice for him to get an ego boost like that.

When I confronted him with the fact that their relationship was destructive to both of them, to her because she pined for him, and to him because he needed to look for this reassurance in himself or from someone in the "present," his response was that maybe he really would marry her someday. But as soon as he said it, he admitted that she was really not the right one for him. It took me a long time to get him to see that having this old incomplete relationship was like a back door escape hatch that was keeping him from committing fully to relationships right in front of him—that she was his security blanket. He finally ended up calling her and telling her that he couldn't call her anymore and the reasons why. But he says that he still gets this urge to call her after a particularly bad date. It will probably take a lot of willpower, but by clearing his slate, he is strengthening his own ability to commit to another relationship.

Almost everyone has old "dangling" relationships that are neither "active" nor "complete." If you just look through your address book, you might pick out many people who fall into this category. They may include people you have had very serious relationships with that didn't end 100 percent, of whom you are always thinking, "Someday, maybe we'll get together." Or maybe there's that person you call when you can't get another date, hoping that maybe this time when you go out you might see something in him or her you had never seen before. Or there could be someone that you have dated off and on for a long time. Or there may just be someone you like who isn't "the one." The point is, you need to get these people out of your life!

People hold onto these "dangling" relationships as security blankets, otherwise there would be . . . no one. That's right! In order to have someone special fill you up to the brim, there can be *no one* else there taking up the room! If you need someone to talk to late at night to console you after a hard date, start making new friends! Old love relationships turning into simple friendships may in very rare circumstances work, but, for the majority of cases, they simply keep people stuck in the past. As long as there is even one last vestige of hope that one of these people will miraculously turn into "Mr. or Ms. Right," you will not be fully committed to working hard to find the real "Mr. or Ms. Right." That means that there mustn't be one single "dangling" name left in your address book! One of the single most powerful things you can do to find a mate is to start your search with a clean slate.

The process might be simple, or take more time and effort. For relationships that weren't that significant or important to you, it may just be as simple as very deliberately, with a black magic marker, crossing those people's names out of your address book forever. This will only be possible if you know that doing this will really complete it for you, and that you won't think about them again after you cross them out. For more meaningful relationships, in order to really end them, you probably need to personally communicate your intentions. This can be difficult, but think about the fact that if you are holding onto them, they must also be holding onto you in the same way. And by ending "nowhere" relationships, you are also doing your former partners a big favor because they can now start their search with a clean slate also.

To accomplish this, you can communicate with former partners by telephone, or if you find that too difficult, by writing them notes. When you communicate with someone, don't be too significant or self-righteous, just say in your own words that you are simply calling to let the person know that you appreciate all that you have been to each other, but you are serious now about finding someone to marry, and that you are going through your address book to complete all past relationships to kind of "clean the slate." Let that person say whatever he or she has to say, but whatever that person does, *do not let him or her invalidate* what you are doing! They may be rude, or laugh, or even be hurt, but one thing is for sure, you will gain an enormous amount of freedom from this process. And believe it or not, it will make an impression on them—not only that you are a powerful, determined person, but also that maybe they should be doing the same thing. (Of course, they probably won't tell you this.)

Even if you write a note telling someone these things, make sure to give the person the opportunity to write or call you back. Listening is part of the completion process for you, otherwise you will wonder whether the person got the letter or not, or what he or she thought, and it will still be "dangling." However, if you write a note, and the person doesn't respond, then that is fine, consider it complete. Then take your trusty black marker and cross that person out of your address book forever!

If someone won't take no for an answer, find out why. Just because you have a history with this person doesn't make you obligated to be a friend to him or her for life. Listen to this person, even talk to him or her over time, in different discussions about where you are coming from. But be firm in what you want to accomplish. If this person values your friendship so much, and you also enjoy this person's company, (I do not recommend this), tell him or her that you will only remain friends under the following conditions: that the relationship must be 100 percent platonic, with no variance from this ever, and that the two of you must understand that there is *no hope* of it ever becoming romantic. If you sense, even a little (and you must be very honest with yourself here), that either of you would remain hopeful that it would one day turn into something else, but not lead to marriage, then cut your losses short and do yourself the favor of ending it *now*.

Also, if any of the people you crossed off your address list that you never contacted call you, then at that time you must also express to them where you stand on the issue, and that you do not want to see them because you are starting your life with a clean slate. Do not feel as if you need to justify yourself to them. You are working on the most important project of your life—who cares if they understand it or like it?

Step Four: Make Room for This Project

The fourth step, which is kind of fun, is to clear a spot in your apartment or house that is designated as the area dedicated to the project of getting married. Pick a place that is special, like the top drawer of your dresser, the right-hand side of your roll-top desk, or even a certain corner on top of your work space. You need to have plenty of room so you don't have to shuffle everything around all the time to access it. What you keep in this location is this book, any and all books you are reading on the subject (either on getting married, or self-help books to forward the project of your emotional preparation), any personal ad information, incoming personal ad mail, your list of what you are looking for in a mate (see Chapter 3), advice to yourself or from others on index cards (which you can also carry with you), and any other items or articles that relate to this project. The purpose of this is twofold: one is to keep all of the information orderly and together, and the other is so that the physical presence of this material will keep the project "alive" for you.

The work outlined in this chapter will not only take determination, but will also take time. These steps will not get taken by themselves, and the longer you put them off, the more they will hang over you. You may feel as if you are not quite ready to take these projects on, but you truly never will feel quite ready. The secret is to take action—your feelings will eventually catch up with you, and the movement forward created by taking action will inspire you to forge ahead! You will be more full of life and determination than you ever thought possible!

NOTEBOOK

1. The first step is to rid yourself of all items that scream out, "Single person lives here!" Items you still need to get rid of:

_____

_____

_____

2. The second step is to throw away all old photographs of past relationships. What made it hard for you to do this?

_____

_____

_____

3. Now that you have thrown them all away, how do you feel?

_____

_____

_____

4. Now throw away all old mementos of past relationships, and throw or give away all gifts from past relationships. Gift items you still need to get rid of:

_____

_____

_____

5. How does this "cleaning house" make you feel?

_____

_____

_____

_____

6. The third step is to cross out all nonsignificant old "dangling" relationships from your address book. Make a list of those people with whom you need to communicate before you cross them off in your address book. Include the date by when you will call them:

Name: By when:

_____   _____

_____   _____

_____   _____

_____   _____

_____   _____

_____   _____

_____   _____

_____   _____

_____   _____

_____   _____

_____   _____

7. Are you complete with all past relationships, and do you truly have a clean slate?

_____

_____

_____

_____

8. How does being complete make you feel?

_____

_____

_____

_____

9. Designate a spot in your home for the project of getting married. Are you more committed to getting married now than at any previous time in your entire life? If not, what's stopping you from this commitment?

_____

_____

_____

_____

3

Making a List

THIS IS THE PART where everyone turns to mush. People are scared to set down definitive guidelines as to what they are looking for in their mates for fear that this will make it impossible to find them. This is an exact contradiction to logical thinking. How can you find something if you don't know what you're looking for? This is where the skilled, "been single a long time" intelligentsia pipes up: "Well, I'll know it when I find it." This phrase has caught on as though it makes sense. What has it got you in the past? More of the same old patterns that you are now working so hard to break! Do not be so trusting of your instinct about these things. You are taking chances with the whole rest of your life. Be smart. Think about what you are looking for. Be specific. Do not settle for anything less than what you want. Yes, it might be possible for you to accidently run into someone who is "perfect" for you, but the odds are greatly against it.

Now, you may feel that you could be happy with anyone, that you could somehow make it all work. You are welcome to believe this, but considering the staggering divorce rates, I'd rather take my chances and look for someone who is as compatible with me as possible. Whether there is only one person out there who is "the one" is impossible to say, but even if this were true, you would still need to know what you are looking for when you find that special someone.

The other problem that gets in the way of being clear on what we need in a mate is a familiar phenomenon known as "falling in love." Most of us grew up thinking that one day destiny would somehow take over, that we wouldn't even have to think, that the perfect mate would suddenly appear in our lives.

This is one of the primary reasons many people are afraid to take any real action toward finding a mate; they are afraid they will "jinx" fate. But somehow the fantasy never comes true for them. They keep wishing and hoping, but suffer one great disappointment after another. If only they would realize that what is at the heart of their "falling in love" is not destiny at all, but their own old dysfunctional patterns. Putting your entire future in the hands of your emotions may be fun, but it is not a reliable way to find someone who will make you happy. The only way to make sure that you "fall in love" with someone who meets your needs is to make a list of your needs . . . and resolve only to love someone who meets those needs.

Again, the proof is in the pudding. When you have your list honed down to a clear picture of what you are looking for, the clarity that your search takes on will astound you. Your job will simply be to match people to your list. If a person doesn't match, it is such a relief not to spend agonizing nights wondering if this person could possibly turn into "the one" with a little work, or to try to change your personality to one that you think will fit this particular person better. All of that will be behind you, and you can just relax and be yourself.

Step One: Make a Master List

The first step is to begin making a list of what you are looking for in a mate. At first, your list will be fairly vague. It is important to start somewhere, and later you can take your time to hone this list to the most important items to you. I was speaking to two roommates, Alan and Brian, who said that they were very reluctant to make a list. Not only did they both feel that it was too "contrived," but that they were better off going with their "gut instincts." After a very long discussion, what finally got through to them was that they both admitted that they already did have a list, only it was subconscious. It was made up of "Hollywood" images, old dysfunctional patterns, and the right "feeling of chemistry." Both of them saw that it would never truly get them a healthy relationship. So we spent a lot of time just getting the lists started. I wish I had taken a picture of Brian's gleeful face when he came up with the terms "tender" and "enthusiastic" to describe his future mate!

To start your list, write down everything that comes to your mind. Even write down unimportant items just to get them out of your head and onto paper. Do this right now in your notebook at the end of this chapter even before you go on to step two. Items might include: attractive, sense of humor, trustworthy, strong family values, loves to talk, isn't too serious . . . .

Step Two: Dismantle the Pictures

The second step is to begin to dismantle your "pictures" of the "ideal" mate. Those ideals are likely the very things that keep you from finding a person that meets all of your *needs*, versus someone who fills all your *wants*. This distinction is very important. If you ask happy, long-married couples what the most important qualities are in their mates, their lists will be about items that meet people's needs, not about what those people wanted at a fleeting moment in time twenty years ago when they got married. An example of a want is someone who looks like a model; an example of a need is someone who is thoughtful and caring.

The big problem is that American society is based on wants. If you read the personal columns, it is so amusing to see people list absolutely ridiculous wants one after another! They think getting those things will make them happy! What does the fact that someone loves to walk on the beach have to do with whether he or she is a good mate or not? Is that what one *needs* to be happy? Rarely do you read about someone who writes what his or her needs are. Although you may not know what your needs are, don't make the mistake of chasing after your wants. Think about what you really need.

Dismantling your pictures of the ideal mate means examining all of your own wants, and seeing if they really are so important. If you could trade all of your wants for getting what you really need, wouldn't you do it? Wouldn't it be amazing if you really received all the emotional support, love, tenderness, kindness, and caretaking that you really need? How can your wants ever hold a candle to what is possible for you when you look for someone who meets all of your needs?

Lynn told me that there was something definitely wrong with her. She said that she was going out with a man who was everything that she ever wanted. He was handsome, dressed well, and had a very active social life, which she had become a part of in the four months since they had started dating. He was secure in his career, played tournament tennis, and was what she called "the perfect catch." But she was not happy in the relationship. She said that maybe she just wasn't used to having a healthy relationship.

I asked her if she had talked to him at all about this. She replied that he really didn't like to talk about things that much. I asked her what she meant, and she said that he told her that he was a "doer." He felt that if you had to talk about the relationship, it couldn't be that good. Just being together and enjoying each other is what makes a successful relationship.

I asked her how she felt about this. Lynn said that he must be right because his parents were still married after thirty-four years, and her folks divorced when she was fourteen. He must know a lot more about solid relationships than she does. I repeated my question about how she felt about his philosophy. She looked at me, and said that it made her sad. As wonderful as he was, the thought of spending the rest of her life with no one to talk to made her feel very lonely.

Again she repeated that there must be something very wrong with her because she was so needy. I said to her that she was very lucky. She knew something about herself that would make it much easier for her to find a husband. She now knew that she needed to have a husband with whom she could communicate fully. A huge smile came across her face, and she said that having a husband like that would be a miracle for her.

Instead of being a victim of circumstances, she became determined to get what she needed. Her first step, she said, was to talk to her current boyfriend and to tell him what her needs were to see if he could accommodate them. If not, she said that communication was more important to her than having the perfect catch.

Look over your own list. Examine the items that fall into the want category. Feel free to cross any items off, and add others. Begin writing down items that you think you really need. Also, even before we cover the topic of values fully, start thinking about the role that values play in a successful, healthy relationship. Similar values can make even difficult times easier to deal with, and are a good strong base for a family and for raising children. While you are thinking about and writing down some of your needs, begin to jot down some of your values, and indicate which values you need your spouse to share.

Step Three: Get Beyond Materialism

The third step is to learn how to get beyond materialism. This is no easy task. Materialism is taught to us long before our ABC's. It is in every part of our daily lives, and the accumulation of material wealth has become the "purpose" of many people's lives. If you think back to the last car you got, or any other big item, you can probably clearly remember the elation you felt as you drove down the street. In fact, the harder you worked for this item, the more excitement you probably experienced. This then became strong motivation to work harder and to get more "things." We also by nature want to have things to impress our friends and feel like we are worthy people and have "made it." Thus we are left with a society that literally revolves around the accumulation of material goods.

The question you need to ask yourself is what do you really want from life? How long did the elation from that new car last? If you were given the choice of finding a loving, caring, devoted partner, would you forego lots of material goods? If our whole life revolves around materialism, naturally this would be part of your search for a mate. Some people even look for a mate simply as another "material" good. However, it is possible to have both material goods and a devoted partner. As soon as you commit yourself to finding someone with solid values rather than searching for someone from a materialistic point of view, you enter a whole new wonderful world that is so much more rewarding and fulfilling than material goods could ever be. If you have ever eaten dinner at someone's house where the family members are very close and good to each other, you will know for sure that just this simple example alone proves that there is so much more value out there than what one can find in material items.

Your job now is to examine your list to see how much materialism plays in your search, and cross these items off your list. One way to review your list is to compare the traits "must be financially successful" and "must love what he or she does for a living." How do the two compare? When you think of each of your future mates, who would you rather come home to at night, someone who made a lot of money but maybe hated his or her work, or someone who came home energized and enthusiastic about his or her career? Which mate would be a better role model for children? Which one would live life for now, and which one would always be talking about retirement? These are issues you must think about, and realize that what you choose now may have ramifications far into the future.

Step Four: Determine Who You Want to Be
The fourth step is to write down who you want to be in five years. This exercise is fun, and gives you an opportunity to invent a future for yourself that you could really get turned on about! This is fantasy time! Describe everything in great detail: the town you live in, the

home you live in, the kinds of friends you have, the things you do, the family you have, your daily activities, your mate, what you are like, your community involvement, what hobbies you have, the projects you are working on, and what kind of values you have. Write everything down in your notebook as if you were a stranger looking in on the life of someone else.

When you are finished, look over this description and feel the sense of peace that it creates in you. (This warm feeling is similar to what you want to feel when you are with "Mr. or Ms. Right.") Now is the time to look closely at your description and pick out certain points about what you want for your future that would be important for your mate to want also. Add these items to your list in your notebook. This is very helpful, for instance, because if your vision has kids in it, you want to make sure to write that down so you can easily eliminate someone who sees a life of world travel for the future. Your job of eliminating unsuitable mates from your search will thus be much easier for you.

Step Five: Examine Your Values

The fifth step is to begin examining your values. There are two major ways to think about values. The first is in terms of what gives your life meaning, and the second has to do with ethics. Both are very important in terms of what you are looking for in a mate. Before we discuss ethics, it is important for you to start thinking about the question, What gives your life meaning? There are many different answers to this question, but they all fall under three broad categories: social, spiritual, and intellectual fulfillment. They are not mutually exclusive, but it is valuable to look at each of them individually.

For some people, the social aspects of their lives give their lives meaning. Their interactions with their families, friends, or communities give them a purpose to their lives. Taking care of their children makes otherwise mundane daily tasks meaningful and valuable. Entertaining their friends and becoming closer to them year after year gives their lives a sense of continuity and strength. Or working in their communities with the poor or sick gives them a purpose.

Then there are people for whom spirituality gives life meaning. While others are busy running from one appointment to another, they find meaning in taking time out to examine themselves and the world around them. They find strength in the fact that there may be a greater purpose in life than merely living, going through the motions, and dying. Depending on the type of spirituality they practice, whether they adhere to strict religious doctrine or not, they have in common the belief that there is a purpose greater than what is clearly evident.

There are also people whose intellectual pursuits give their lives meaning. This would include people who dedicate their lives to finding the cure for cancer, or people who are determined to invent the next best thing to the light bulb. Some people spend their lives expressing themselves artistically, and yet others commit themselves to saving the trees in the South American rain forests.

Of course, most people do not fit neatly into any one of these categories. However, it is extremely valuable for you to figure out where you stand on these issues. One way to think about it is to give each area certain percentage points depending on how important it is to you. For example, you might get 60 percent social, 25 percent spiritual, and 15 percent intellectual fulfillment and meaning in your life. Take your time to really think this through. The answers you come up with might surprise you. What you thought was really important to you may only be an afterthought when you compare it to some of your other values. You can derive fulfillment from many areas—what you are doing now, which is so important, is prioritizing these values. The answers that you come up with will be very powerful in your search for a mate. Write down your own values in this chapter's notebook section.

Once you see which areas are most important to you, think about which values you are looking for in a mate. Doug told me that he found most of his satisfaction in life from his intellectual pursuits. As an academic researcher, he had a mission that was so exciting that sometimes he couldn't wait to get to work in the morning. He had dated a woman from his lab for two years who also derived her meaning in life from these pursuits. But neither person felt that he or she was "the one" for the other, so they broke up. I told Doug that the key is not if you and your mate have the same values, but rather if you have "complementary" values. We talked more about his life, and he said that one of his big regrets is that he doesn't have many close friends, or any social life. We discussed the possibility that maybe he should put down on his list someone who has a high percentage of social values. This would complement his life very nicely.

Write down the values that you are looking for in a mate that you think will best be suited to your own values. This may be hard to do, but remember, they are just guidelines to assist you in finding someone who is compatible. As you search for a mate, try to discern where the person fits in these categories. It might be hard to judge, but talking to your prospective partner about what is most important to him or her is a good way to find out. Someone who talks a lot about his or her family probably falls into the social category. Also remember that a person's values do change a bit over time, but one person can rarely change another person's values.

It is also important to examine for a moment some of the "false" meanings in life that people pursue, either out of ignorance, or because they mistakenly believe that fulfillment of these areas will lead to fulfillment of the three aforementioned "purposes" in life. A sampling of false meanings might be the pursuit of fame, power, money or materialism, looking good, or reckless "fun." Unfortunately, there are a great many people who pursue these things. You need to learn to recognize these types of people so that you don't waste many precious years of your life chasing after these false purposes.

A Look at Ethics

Now we can take a look at the other major way to think about values, which is in terms of ethics. Obviously, everyone wants to marry someone with good ethics. Someone who has integrity, keeps his or her promises, doesn't say bad things about other people, doesn't lie, does what he or she says he or she will do, is honest in financial affairs, doesn't try to get away with petty dishonesties, works very hard to be fair and just, and stands up for what he or she believes is right. These characteristics we can all agree on. The problem is, how do you know whether someone has these characteristics or not?

Most people try to judge someone's ethical standards by trying to see whether that person is running an embezzling scam or not. That's not the place to look. As with many things, simple actions speak the loudest. Ask yourself if your date keeps his or her word. Does he or she always break dates? If he or she offhandedly brags about lying to someone about something, make note of it. Watch how your date reacts when someone else is treated unjustly. Does he or she laugh at the "sucker"? See if your date cuts in long lines and tries to get everything from "the system." These little actions will tell you more about a person than anything that person says about "honesty." And beware of your own desire to overlook these things. People see what they want to see. Remember that you will have to live with these things for a long time. And, if you are interested in having children, no matter how much you tell them about correct ethics and moral standards, children mimic what their parents do, not what they say. Choose a partner wisely with this in mind.

Step Six: Make a Top Ten List

The sixth step is to narrow your list down to ten items. *What?!* After all the work you've just done! This work has been very important, and not one ounce of it is wasted. It is just that the next very valuable part of the process is to work out your priorities in terms of what you are looking for in a spouse. This is going to force you to choose between very important values and needs of yours. You are going to have to make some tough decisions and ask yourself what things you simply cannot live without.

The paring down process may take you some time to do—days or weeks of evaluating and mulling over your priorities. But by making the kinds of decisions you need to make to narrow down your list, you are using the same muscle you're going to need to decide whether someone is right for you or not. You certainly need this practice! This is one of the most productive processes you can follow to not only make sure that you get married, but that you marry the right person!

My friend Jamie said that she had eleven items on her list. She just couldn't eliminate one of the last two priorities: that he be kind and thoughtful. The way we resolved this issue is by thinking through the two attributes. If a person were truly thoughtful of another person, that person probably couldn't help but be kind. That person would want to treat another with kindness and concern. Whereas, if a person were kind, he or she might not necessarily always be thoughtful. So to avoid redundancy, and to narrow down the list, Jamie took "being kind" off her list.

This process begins to shape what your mate will be like. It becomes so clear that when you have your final list, you can almost feel your mate's presence in the room! It is very exciting, and will make your dating process so pain free. You are now clear on what you are looking for—if someone doesn't match your list, it will be obvious to you. Just carry your list with you on the date (in your mind please, let's not be tacky!), and instead of engaging in the usual small talk and seeing whether the two of you have "chemistry" or not, you will spend your time talking and finding out if that person is what you are looking for. No more wondering, acting chameleon-like to get approval, or berating yourself for not being a certain way that you think might be more attractive. You now have the freedom to totally be yourself!

You may be concerned because people have said to you that the reason you aren't married is because you are too critical of people. But there is a big difference between being critical and being clear. It is easy to go on a date and pick a person apart piece by piece. People are full of foibles and weaknesses and have many characteristics that may not be to our liking. What is valuable and necessary is to try to see what kind of person he or she really is. When you used to go on your dates armed with your old list full of wants and "Mr. or Ms. Hollywood" criteria, you could sum someone up in just one glance. Casting someone off for all of the superficial reasons that used to be important to you is what people mean when they say the reason you aren't married is because you are too critical of people. This is not what you are doing when you go on dates with your new list. Now you are working hard by talking to this person to see if the two of you have the same values and visions for your lives. You aren't looking for "Mr. or Ms. Perfect," you are just looking for someone who is right for you.

I had the privilege to talk to both sides of a blind date after they had spent an evening together. Blake was very interested in pursuing Jill, but Jill, who I had spoken to many times on the telephone about relationships, was not interested. Jill told me that she was sure that Blake liked her just for her looks and because she was clear on what she wanted for her future. But he didn't even match two of the items on her list. He wasn't spiritually oriented, didn't talk at all about his family, wasn't open when she asked him how he felt about communication in a relationship, and talked a lot about his material goals for the coming year. She was absolutely clear that he was not right for her.

Blake, on the other hand, told me that Jill was very nice, pretty, and seemed to have a good head on her shoulders. But these characteristics he selected don't have much to do with how compatible the two would be. I spent some time talking to Blake about making a top ten list so that he could spend his dates productively. One of the first conclusions that he came up with is that it's more important to him that his mate be caring than pretty.

And remember to keep in mind that once you find this person, this person may not look or seem like what you think he or she should look or seem like. In other words, even when you know exactly what you want, when you find someone right, it is likely that he or she will be difficult for you to recognize. That is because even once you have your list, the human mind cannot help but create "pictures" of someone, and those pictures may be hard for you to see beyond.

When Peter met Alice, he knew right away that she was "the one" for him. And even though he matched seven of the items on her list, Alice just didn't feel he was for her. He just didn't match her "picture" of "Mr. Right." But Peter kept persisting and asked her out again and again even though she turned him down many times, and was less than enthusiastic when she said yes. But after seven months of irregular dating, Alice started to recognize in Peter a quality that she never saw before—someone who was totally devoted to her. This frightened her at first, but she soon grew to depend on Peter. After another four months of dating, he proposed to her, and she accepted!

After making your list, and after meeting "the one" (even if he or she doesn't seem like it), hopefully the power of this connection will bring the two of you together one way or another. Also remember that there is a big difference between compromising and settling. Compromising is when you say, "Well, this person has seven out of ten of the items on my list, and I really think that we will be happy together." And settling is giving up your search after three months because it doesn't seem to be working, and the person you are currently dating isn't so bad after all. (Never mind that this person doesn't match any of the items on your list, isn't serious about ever getting married to you, and reinforces all of your old patterns that you are trying so hard to put behind you.)

To find the mate that you have always wanted to have, you must be determined and persistent. You may have bad months where it all looks hopeless, but don't let anything stand in your way! Even if you have to stick it out for a whole year, or even two! (Although often once you are clear on what you are looking for it happens surprisingly quickly.) But wouldn't you give a year of your life to find the best mate on the planet for you that you can spend the rest of your life with? You will only live one time on earth, and you deserve to have the best life possible! And, if you do get discouraged, talk to a friend, or reread this book to reinspire you to get back on track.

There is one last thing that you must be warned about. Few people really know what they want in life. Those who do are extremely attractive to others. Now that you know what you are looking for, when you go out on dates, you will be a lot more attractive to people. This is wonderful, but it will make your search much more difficult because the people that you go out with will often want to go on a second date with you to pursue the relationship. This will be enticing to you, but you must remember that if you know that a person is not "the one," or potentially "the one," *do not go out with that person again!* Yes it is a nice stroke to your ego, but you must keep meeting as many people as you can and not waste any time if you want to find who you are looking for.

NOTEBOOK

1. The first step is to make a list of what you are looking for in a mate. Jot down everything that comes to your mind. (This is your first draft to be edited later.)

_____

_____

_____

_____

_____

_____

_____

_____

_____

_____

_____

_____

_____

_____

_____

_____

_____

_____

_____

_____

_____

2. The second step is to look over your list and to cross off all items that fall into the "want" category, and to add items that fall into the "need" category.

3. The third step is to learn how to get beyond materialism. Cross off items that fall into the materialism category.

4. Write down who you want to be in five years. (Who, what, where, when, and how . . . let your fantasies go wild!)

_____

_____

_____

_____

_____

_____

_____

_____

_____

_____

5. The fifth step is to begin examining your values. Write down your own values, and then add to your list in question 1 the complementary values that you are looking for in a mate.

_____

_____

_____

_____

_____

_____

_____

_____

6. The sixth step is to narrow your list down to ten items:

1. _____   6. _____

2. _____   7. _____

3. _____   8. _____

4. _____   9. _____

5. _____   10. _____

4

Making a Plan

MOST PEOPLE HATE PLANS. Plans get in the way of real living, and put constraints and obligations on everything you do. Not only that, plans are incredibly hard to write, most of the goals are "pie in the sky," and sticking to a plan is just about impossible. So why are they so touted by professional "consultants" as *the* way to succeed? Why are they part of every corporation's business, every organization's bylaws, every Olympic athlete's daily life, and the vast majority of successful people's way of living? What is it about this device called a plan that has the whole world singing its praises?

The answer is simple. A plan has the power to create the future. Even for a simple task such as doing the dishes, you start with a simple plan of taking dirty dishes, washing them, and trying to accomplish the result of a pile of clean, dry dishes. If an ancient tribesman were to come across the pile of dirty dishes, his plan might be to use them as projectile devices to render an animal unconscious. It is easy to see that, depending on the intended result, very different actions take place. A plan starts by determining the result to be produced, and then takes a step-by-step approach to accomplishing that result. It answers the questions: What do you want to accomplish? How do you want to accomplish it? By when do you want to accomplish it?

As an example of how planning works, think about the last time you were in a retail store for a post-holiday sale. There are two hundred customers squirming around in a tiny little shop, an inventory that looks like a tornado just hit, and only one sales clerk with a bad attitude standing behind the counter. The owner of this store did not have good planning ability. If he or she did, he or she would have spread the sale over many days to avoid two hundred customers at once, and he or she would have trained five additional clerks to assist with the cashiering, two of whom could straighten out the inventory to increase visibility and thus sales.

The owner did not stop to think about the end result that he or she was looking for as a store owner, to sell as much merchandise as possible at as high a profit as possible. The way to accomplish this (the owner's plan) would be to get as much foot traffic in the store as possible, increase the number of loyal customers, have a neat looking shop to be able to sell higher priced items, have good service, and make the store a pleasant place to shop.

Obviously, the shop owner did not accomplish any of these items. Like most people, the owner was just focusing on a short-term goal, in this case, trying to get rid of excess holiday inventory. The owner didn't realize that in the process he or she was alienating all of the customers. In fact, this store owner was acting in direct contradiction to what the intended result for the business is. Yes, by hiring more workers the profits on this sale would have been lower, but by having many more satisfied customers, the business would have done much better in the future. The moral of the story is that by having a solid plan and sticking to it, you don't focus so much on intermediate short-term goals, you think more about the long run and what your intended result is.

This is very important in your search for a mate. A plan will keep you on track during the emotional turbulence that dating engenders. It doesn't matter how mature and strong you are, searching for a mate is a difficult process. When things get tough, your plan will be there for you. Instead of sulking, you just go on to the next step of your plan. There is nothing like action to get your enthusiasm for the project back in line! And, you are expressing your own power to create your own future, a future that otherwise would not happen without you making it happen.

How to Meet Mr. or Ms. Right

The process of creating a plan is to start by determining what you want to accomplish. This you have already done in Chapter 3 with your list of what you are looking for in a mate. The last part of creating a plan is to determine by when you want to accomplish this. You have already done this in Chapter 1, step one. (Isn't plan making easy!) Now the only step left is to determine how you want to accomplish it.

The first thing that you must realize is that finding a mate is a numbers game. The more potentials you meet, the greater your odds of finding "the one." It would be much easier if you could enjoy a couch potato life and have your ideal mate come find you. Many people are very experienced at this "plan" of finding a mate. Unfortunately, it doesn't have a very good track record! The plan that does have a good track record is *getting out there*. This may be hard for some people, but it works. I am not talking about the "single's scene" at bars, I am talking about taking a quiet life that revolves around getting home from work, getting a bite to eat, catching a TV show, and going to sleep, and turning it into one that is filled with many outside activities.

I have a friend who wants to get married but keeps telling me over and over again the story of how her parents met. Her mother was sitting at home reading a book on the porch. Her father, who was visiting someone on her street, came to the wrong house and fate put the two of them together. She has a very strong conviction that fate plays the biggest role in one's destiny. Whether this is true or not, at forty-two, she needs to at least try to help fate along a bit. Even her mother helped fate along by being *out there*. If she had been inside her house, the stranger would have walked up the steps, seen the house number, and gone on his way. Unfortunately, I still don't think I convinced my friend to help fate along. I don't know how she can be so attached to her own belief system that she's willing to just sit around and wait. Maybe she is right, but I wouldn't take that chance if I were she.

Outside activities are not only the ideal place to meet a mate, but, by participating, you are at the same time making yourself a more rounded, desirable person who would make a good mate for someone. The interests that you pursue, and the activities that you take up, will be very enriching to your life. And if you meet someone at these activities, you already have something in common, something to do together, and something that you can share even after you are married.

There are many ways to "get out there," and all of them do not involve activities, but the following list will get you started. You may have tried these same activities before and failed; it is now time to try again. Before, you were looking for all the wrong things, and probably were resigned that nothing would work. Turn over a new leaf and start again with new determination, enthusiasm, and a commitment to getting the job done this time!

Of course you shouldn't plan to do everything in the following list, that would be setting yourself up for failure. Just pick out two to five items that seem like they would work best for you. A lot depends on your personality and what you like to do, and a lot depends on what kind of a mate you are looking for. Get active in areas that you are interested in. There is no sense trying to find a mate at a baseball game if you hate sports. As you read through the listing, start jotting in your notebook different ideas and places that you want to investigate. When you are done with that list, we will go back over it and organize that information into a "plan."

Networking

Networking is by far the best way to meet your mate. The way you do this is to tell everyone you know that you want to get married. If you are embarrassed, do it anyway. Even tell people exactly what you are looking for (using your list to guide you). Tell them that you are open to being given phone numbers, or fixed up on blind dates. Tell them you only want to go out with people who are serious about getting married. Tell them you know that the best way for you to find someone is to spread the word, and that they are welcome to help you spread the word, too.

Then tell every person you meet (that you may not even know!) that you want to get married. This includes people at social gatherings, acquaintances at work, a friend of a friend, and even your hairdresser. You never know around which corner "the one" might be waiting! The more people that are in on this with you, the greater your odds of finding that special person.

The way that I met my husband is by telling a perfect stranger not only that I wanted to get married, but by when, and exactly what I was looking for! By that time, I had been avidly "getting out there" for over seven months. But I was also particular and clear about what I was looking for. There is a big difference between being desperate and being determined. All I was interested in was being introduced to as many people as possible so that I could find "the one." And I did!

Also, don't forget to thank every person who helped you out in any way. Whether someone gives you someone's phone number, calls someone's sister for you, sets you up with his or her brother, or even tells you where the best place to meet people is, that person deserves some appreciation. Don't be one of those rude people who is so disappointed by a blind date that you not only never respond to let the fixer-upper know how it went, but avoid that person at all costs. What those poor souls don't realize is that there is no one more willing and determined to fix them up with their right partners as someone who has erred in the past! Take good care of your supporters.

Volunteering

Volunteering is also one of the best ways to meet someone great. First of all, you know that whoever you meet is probably going to be a pretty decent person if he or she is giving time to a worthy cause. This is not always the case, but often people who are active in the community are there because they care. Concern for others is a very good trait, and incredibly valuable to a family. Plus, when you are working side by side with someone on a "cause," you learn many things about that person that you can't see in a singles setting. How does this person react to time pressures? How does he or she treat fellow volunteers? How does he or she handle frustration? How is this person's sense of humor? Anyone sitting on a bar stool can talk a lot about what a great person he or she is, but get that person into the thick of a situation, and he or she can't put on too much of an act.

Ed told me the story of when he first met his girlfriend Luana. They had dated a few times, and he liked her, but she just seemed to be waiting to be entertained. Then he brought her to one of the fundraising events he was working on, and her whole personality changed. She got right into the action, working fast and furiously on each project she was given to do. He even caught a glimpse of her laughing heartily when she dropped a stack of envelopes.

When they went out for coffee afterward, Ed asked Luana what created such a change. She was surprised at his initial impression of her as a quiet person. She said that maybe because she was an accomplished professional woman, on their first dates she just didn't want to come on too strong. Their ability to talk about these intimate areas will assist them in having a stronger relationship together, but it was the "getting out there" that truly helped Ed to see this woman for who she really was—someone who, Ed confessed, might just be "Ms. Right."

To find the best volunteer group to participate in, think about what your interests are. It might be hard to pick one off the top of your head, but once you start gathering information in Chapter 5, you will find out where to dig up lists of organizations to select one that is just waiting for you to join. For finding a mate, joining a "doing" organization is probably the best way to get to know people. Volunteering by sitting on a board is very nice, but you don't get around as much or meet as many people.

Personal Ads

Personal ads really do work. Even though people do write in their list of wants, it is valuable to have a large number of single people listed in one place who are serious about having relationships. Try to overlook the way the ads focus on the superficial, and find someone whose ad sparks your interest. Since personal ads are such a big part of our culture, many good people are turning to this resource, and you can meet some quality people by scanning your local paper's pages.

Answering ads is fun, and it gives you the power to select someone you think is interesting. But by far the most exciting part of personal ads is writing an ad of your own. Not only is it a valuable experience to have to write down who you are and what you are looking for in very few words, but there is nothing like having a tough day at the office and coming home to a mailbox full of people who want to meet you! To write your ad, take your list of what you are looking for in a mate, pick the most vital issues, and word them so that they are clear and not too demanding. Also, write a few choice adjectives about yourself that are a bit more meaningful than what you typically find in the ads. The point of an ad is to narrow down who contacts you, and to attract the kinds of people that you want to meet. Don't worry if your ad's not perfect. As long as it fits who you are, then it should work just fine.

When you are screening your responses, always try to have a lengthy phone conversation with each person before meeting him or her. See if your prospective mate matches the items on your list, and without prejudging too much, make sure that you are using your time effectively. And women should be very careful to meet dates in a public meeting place that they have been to before to make sure that they are safe. This person is a stranger to you, and you can never be too careful.

One man said that he had tried personal ads and he never met anyone even close to what he was looking for. To him, they were just a waste of time. I advised him to forget about personal ads. (With his attitude he'd never find anyone through them!) But I think he's making a mistake by passing up a good source of dates. Personal ads may not have been a successful source for him for many reasons.

Maybe he didn't give them enough of a chance. Who knows whether his very next date might have been a perfect match? Maybe he didn't write an ad that described himself accurately enough so he attracted the wrong types of people. Or maybe he judged his dates from his list of wants instead of needs, and passed up someone who would have made a great partner for him but he couldn't recognize. Who knows, but it certainly would be easy enough for him to give it another try.

Matchmaker, Matchmaker

Using a matchmaker is not only a good idea, it is an absolute necessity in your search. Given that finding a mate is a numbers game, you need to be going out with at least one to two new dates per week (or more)! This is the only way to accomplish your mission. There are many people who find this idea absolutely deplorable, and Chapter 6 will give you some ways to make this process more bearable. But the fact is that *getting out there* not only means meeting people, but spending time with them so that you aren't just judging them by their looks and by what you think of them on your first impression (the worst way possible to pick a mate).

If you are a man, when you meet someone who has even three items right on your list, invite her for a date right away. Don't trust your judgment on whether she'd be right for you or not, spend at least a few hours with her first. If you are a woman, the same applies, if you meet someone who has three items right on your list, either ask him out, or make it clear to him that you would like to get together sometime. The problem is that, for both men and women, this process will create "rejections." And it could make it very hard for you to ask out the next interesting person who comes along. It is hard to keep pursuing people in the face of the fear that they will say no. If you date one hundred people before you find your mate, that means ninety-nine nos! That is why you need a matchmaker.

Matchmakers are wonderful. Just when you are discouraged and want to give up, a matchmaker will call you with the name of someone who sounds fabulous. Matchmakers keep you on your toes, and as their clientele have been prescreened, you know you are meeting someone who already has a lot in common with you. They sometimes make mistakes, but by and large you will meet quality people and accomplish your mission of meeting as many people as possible. And remember that no date is *ever* wasted. You always learn more about yourself, more about what you don't want, and there are so many instances when the wrong date introduced someone to his or her future mate!

Don't leave this very important resource out of the picture. Yes, you are determined to get married, but even a slew of personal ad responses that come in the mail must be phoned and followed up on. You can keep putting this off and jeopardize your future by doing so, but a matchmaker will be persistent with you. Obviously, you need to be persistent, too, but with a matchmaker on your "team," you have a much better chance to succeed.

Matchmakers can also make good confidants. Elizabeth related her experience with a matchmaker to me. She said that she was asked out a lot by people at her gym, and by people at the community center at which she volunteered. But only on rare occasions did she get asked out on a second date. This made her feel bad about herself, but she kept telling herself that when the right man came along, it would all work out, and at least new people kept asking her out.

It wasn't until she went to a matchmaker, however, that she finally found out what was stopping people from asking her out on a second date. Her matchmaker always made it a point to follow up on each date and to find out what each person thought. Her matchmaker relayed to her that the men she fixed her up with all said that while she was very interesting and attractive, she spent the entire first date telling them all of her problems. They said that it was almost as if she was trying to push them away. Elizabeth was shocked. She admitted that she did talk a lot on her dates, but she just wanted the men to get to know her. She saw this as letting her hair down and communicating fully.

Her matchmaker told her that there would be plenty of time to get to know someone fully, but it takes time. Telling someone all about your intimate personal life on the first date just isn't appropriate and puts people off, and being honest doesn't mean "letting it all hang out." She told Elizabeth to tell her problems to her friends, and first dates don't qualify as friends! Her matchmaker advised her to concentrate instead on *listening* on her first dates. Elizabeth told me that after that conversation with her matchmaker, her whole dating world changed, and she was going on second and third dates!

Religious Sanctuaries

One excellent way to meet your mate is through a church or synagogue. Whether you grew up religiously or not, marrying someone of the same religion gives you a common background that cannot be replaced by any other common ground. The histories that your ancestors have in common make the two of you compatible in a way that is deeper than can be simply understood. Many people snub this idea, often as a way of rejecting parental pressure. But the fact remains that same religion marriages fare much better statistically than intermarriages do.

The best way to become active is to find a church or synagogue that has events and classes that are geared for people of your same age group. At these events, become active in what is going on and get to know the people. You are not there to just "check out the scene," which will never result in your finding your mate. If you are to meet your mate in this way, it is likely that you will need to be involved in the organization for many months before you even see this person attending a function. Or that person you've been working on a project with for six weeks could likely be the one to introduce you to his or her niece—who happens to be perfect for you!

Going to services is a good idea, too, and will be spiritually satisfying. If you haven't been in a long time, or are unfamiliar with the procedures, you will feel a lot more comfortable going to events and classes to start you off. And, if after a while you don't feel that this is the place for you, try other churches or synagogues, but be sure to give them each a good, long try. This may take longer than some of the other methods, but your chances of finding someone who is a quality individual, and very suitable for you, are high.

Rachel decided to become active in her local synagogue in order to meet more people. She had never belonged to a synagogue before, but something inside her drew her to make this choice. She not only went to weekly services, she also joined several committees to become active in volunteer work. At first she was intimidated because she felt like an outsider, and because she had a difficult time following the services. But by going regularly, she slowly started to catch on. She told me that from the time she joined the synagogue, her whole life changed. She not only felt a sense of belonging to a community more than she ever had in her life, but the spiritual world gave her a sense of fulfillment which she cherished.

Rachel met and dated many people from her synagogue, but eventually ended up meeting a man at her sister's office. They are now engaged, and are both active at the synagogue. If you give this a try, you might find more than you bargained for.

Classes

Taking classes is not only a good way to meet people, but it gives you the opportunity to grow as well. A long-time great way to meet people, classes offer the advantage of a congenial atmosphere that is very conducive to having private discussions before, during, and after class. It is easy to ask a question about the homework, or to comment on a particular lecture. It also gives you the opportunity to become friendly with someone slowly, over the course of time, which is an incredibly valuable way to get to know someone.

The kinds of people that you meet at classes tend to be interested in the world around them, and in self-growth. These are good traits in a companion. You can also see how serious people are about their commitments, and about doing what they say they are going to do. And, it is also a good place to make friends of the same sex who can introduce you to your future mate.

When you are selecting a class, pick a topic that interests you, but also one that you think that members of the opposite sex will be likely to attend. You probably have some ideas for classes that have been rattling around in your head for years. Well, now is your chance! "The one" could be waiting for you in row three!

Business Associations

Getting involved in business associations is another good way to meet people. The more you get out there, the more likely you are to meet people to date, and to meet people who will introduce you to their friends and associates. The kinds of people you meet at associations, seminars, business events, conventions, and luncheon meetings are all professionals who are interested in their fields. They are not the kinds of people who work nine to five just to get a paycheck. This is a good sign in a partner.

At these events, be as outgoing as you can. Get and give away as many business cards as you can for professional reasons, but also to pursue your goal of finding a mate. This takes a certain amount of finesse because you don't want to come across as unprofessional. Asking someone for a date should be done in a social setting, not in the workplace; and do not ask someone out over whom you have any professional power, since this can be exploitative. Just remember that the person you make advances toward will surely be flattered, and if he or she does turn you down, you have neither lost face professionally nor personally.

Meg, a woman who met her husband at a meeting of a real estate association, said that she had noticed him at a meeting, and then kept going every month to try to meet him. After four months of failure, she finally summoned up the courage to introduce herself. It did not go well at first because he thought she was trying to hone in on a real estate project he was working on. Finally, with nothing to lose, she made it clear that her intentions were purely nonbusiness, and they went together from that day onward. Obviously, she had to experience temporary embarrassment that day, but I bet it was well worth it when she was walking down the aisle!

Sports Clubs

Joining sports clubs and other activity-oriented organizations is an excellent way to meet someone with mutual interests. These clubs also give you something to do together, which is one of the best ways to really get to know someone. If you're hiking through the mountains and someone offers you some of his or her water, that speaks volumes about the person's "caring" qualities. Or if you are bird watching and a person hollers to scare the prize bird away, it says something about the person's sensitivity (or lack thereof). You can tell a lot about people in this way if you are really looking carefully, and if you don't just see what you want to see. Don't be too critical though because if you were to stand back and analyze yourself as an outsider, you also might not be too happy with what you see. Try to be generous and give people the benefit of the doubt if you can. But being active with a group of other people is a great way to learn about people.

Make Your Plan

After you have made your list of areas that you want to pursue, compiled from ideas that you have read here, friends' advice, and ideas that you have come up with yourself, it is time to take this information and make your "plan." The first step is to go over all of these different opportunities and to prioritize them by which item you want to pursue first, which item second, and so forth.

Sometimes it is difficult to decide which to pursue first, but a good rule of thumb is to start with the area that looks most fruitful, even if it is the one you want to start with the least. Often people get discouraged because, in creating their plans, they do the easiest things first and then the rest of the battle is fought uphill. Do yourself a favor by starting with a challenging area. For some that might be writing personal ads, for others it might be joining volunteer groups that they have been considering.

Whatever it is, taking that first step can be exhilarating! You know that finding your mate is now just a matter of time. If it doesn't happen right away, it certainly won't be because of your lack of effort!

Create a "To Do" List

The next step in creating your plan is to organize this information and create a "to do" list for each item on your list. For people who always have great ideas but never follow through on them, the "to do" list is their salvation. Can you imagine carrying the weight of a huge project around with you, wondering where to start, wondering what to do, worried about all that's not getting done, making false starts here and there, but never really accomplishing anything? How discouraging! No wonder so many great ideas get dropped in the middle. The big secret is to break these huge projects into bite-size pieces, to write down all the little things that need to get done, and then to prioritize which ones need to get done first. Then you only have to concentrate on one little item at a time, and when you finish it, it is so rewarding!

Start with the first area on your list that you want to pursue. Write down all the things that need to get done for that item, and then prioritize the list. For instance, to pursue volunteering, you might write down: become a member of a group, research the volunteer groups in my neighborhood, ask Danielle the name of the groups to which she belongs. (Your list will be much longer; this is just an example.) Then when you prioritize, you might put a number 1 in front of researching volunteer groups in your neighborhood because that would be the first step you want to take. Also, as you read through Chapter 5, your to do list may grow and your priorities may change a bit, but it is important to have a working plan even before you start the process of implementation. So go ahead now, in your notebook, and write down all of the things that need to get done for every area on your list. When you are finished, this is your master "plan" for finding a mate! Congratulations!

NOTEBOOK

1. Jot down areas that you want to pursue:

_____   _____

_____   _____

_____   _____

_____   _____

_____   _____

_____   _____

_____   _____

_____   _____

_____   _____

_____   _____

Go over your list and number the items prioritizing them by which item you want to pursue first, which item second, and so forth.

2. Take item number 1 from your list and create a "to do" list for that item. Then put a number beside each item on the to do list in order of priority. Do this for every area on your list above.

ITEM #1:   _____

TO DO LIST:

_____   _____

_____   _____

_____   _____

_____   _____

_____   _____

_____   _____

_____   _____

_____   _____

_____   _____

_____   _____

ITEM #2: _____

TO DO LIST:

_____   _____
_____   _____
_____   _____
_____   _____
_____   _____
_____   _____
_____   _____
_____   _____
_____   _____
_____   _____
_____   _____

ITEM #3: _____

TO DO LIST:

_____   _____
_____   _____
_____   _____
_____   _____
_____   _____
_____   _____
_____   _____
_____   _____
_____   _____
_____   _____
_____   _____
_____   _____

ITEM #4: _____

TO DO LIST:

_____   _____
_____   _____
_____   _____
_____   _____
_____   _____
_____   _____
_____   _____
_____   _____
_____   _____
_____   _____
_____   _____

ITEM #5: _____

TO DO LIST:

_____   _____
_____   _____
_____   _____
_____   _____
_____   _____
_____   _____
_____   _____
_____   _____
_____   _____
_____   _____
_____   _____
_____   _____

ITEM #6:   _____

TO DO LIST:

_____   _____
_____   _____
_____   _____
_____   _____
_____   _____
_____   _____
_____   _____
_____   _____
_____   _____
_____   _____
_____   _____

ITEM #7:   _____

TO DO LIST:

_____   _____
_____   _____
_____   _____
_____   _____
_____   _____
_____   _____
_____   _____
_____   _____
_____   _____
_____   _____
_____   _____
_____   _____

ITEM #8: _____

TO DO LIST:

_____   _____

_____   _____

_____   _____

_____   _____

_____   _____

_____   _____

_____   _____

_____   _____

_____   _____

_____   _____

_____   _____

ITEM #9: _____

TO DO LIST:

_____   _____

_____   _____

_____   _____

_____   _____

_____   _____

_____   _____

_____   _____

_____   _____

_____   _____

_____   _____

_____   _____

_____   _____

ITEM #10:   _____

TO DO LIST:

\# _____   _____

\# _____   _____

\# _____   _____

\# _____   _____

\# _____   _____

\# _____   _____

\# _____   _____

\# _____   _____

\# _____   _____

\# _____   _____

\# _____   _____

5

Implementation

NOW THAT YOU have your plan in hand, it's time to start implementing it! There is nothing as powerful as commitment in action. While it is very important to work on self-development, the main place for you to focus your attention is on your to do list. All of the emotional preparation in the world will not accomplish anything unless accompanied by *action*. Action also produces a miraculous result; your emotional readiness will develop by leaps and bounds simply by moving forward toward your goal.

I am sure that you meet lots of people who want to get married. What have they done that day to accomplish that goal? How about that week, or even that month? The answers you get will probably be pretty uninspiring. What would your answer be? People who accomplish big things often do things that they don't want to do. There will certainly be things that you don't want to do and days that you don't want to even think about getting married. But, your determination and consistency in implementing your plan is *the only thing that is going to make your plan happen!* No one else has the power over your future that you do.

Step One: Getting Started
It is very important to keep in mind the keys to implementing a plan. The *first step* is the most important, and that is: getting started. Even with the best laid-out plans, people have a natural inertia that prevents them from acting on those plans. But remember, it only takes one step to begin the journey, and it is that first vital step that gets the ball rolling. The good part is that it takes a lot less effort

once you have the first few weeks of groundwork done. If you just do one thing each day, the momentum will build, and it will get easier and easier.

Al worked at a large engineering firm. He was an expert at planning and scheduling. His master plan to find a mate was as beautiful as you could imagine. Unfortunately, he was having a very difficult time implementing it. Not only was he very shy, but he had a habit of filling his life with big projects like refinishing his deck or reorganizing his travel slides. These projects always took precedence over his pursuing getting married.

When I talked to Al, I had the feeling that there was absolutely nothing I could say to him that would make any difference. But we continued talking for quite a while, and I think he finally started to realize that everything wasn't going to just "turn out." If he wanted to get married, he was going to have to *make it happen*. He then surprised me by saying that maybe he would try out just one item from his plan, just to get the ball rolling. We both agreed that, given his inertia, his most fruitful place to begin would be with a matchmaker, so that he could be prodded along. Once he got started, it was a lot easier for him to do step two, which was to enroll in a class at a local college.

Step Two: Keep Up the Momentum

The second step is to keep your momentum building no matter how much frustration or hard work you have to put up with. At first, your search will feel like an uphill battle, but be certain that you will get a reward at the end. It's very hard to face constant failure. I remember one week when I went on three blind dates, attended two charity events, put in five hours of volunteer work, and dragged myself to the gym twice, only to come up with nothing and no good prospects.

Those of you who have been through these machinations know the dejected, hopeless feeling you are left with. Somehow if I hadn't tried at all and failed, it wouldn't be so bad. But here I was doing everything in my power to succeed, and I still came up empty-handed. I often felt defeated, and getting back up to bat was always a struggle for me. I guess what helped the most was that I was into so many activities that the momentum worked for me. Just when I was most down, my phone would ring and I would be invited to a volunteer party. Or, I would be home sulking, and someone who had been given my name through my networking efforts would phone me and ask me for a date. I would always force myself to go no matter how I felt. Maybe I wouldn't be at my "best" when I met "Mr. Right," but at least I would meet him! And sometimes, I would even skip an event to sit home and read a good novel. But mostly, I just kept to my plan to get me through the rough times.

You must also keep your momentum building after you have met some good people. Cathy was very enthusiastic and determined to follow her plan thoroughly until she was married. She said that she was going to let nothing stand in her way. But on her fourth date with a man from the personal ads, she changed her tune.

She called me the day after the date and said that she thought she had found "the one." I tried to encourage her to stick to her plan, but she said she wanted to give this relationship all of her energy. So I said that even if he was "the one," that she shouldn't date him exclusively until they were both ready to make that commitment together. I also felt that by dating a lot of other people, she would have the best judgment about whether he was the best mate for her or not. Cathy didn't agree with me, and I didn't hear from her for four months.

When I finally called her to see how everything was going, she had started her plan again. The man she had been dating turned out to be very passive-aggressive, and behind his cool facade he was a very angry person. She told me that she wasn't going to make the mistake again of tossing out her plan. We talked for a long time, and even though I tried, I couldn't hide my frustration about all of the time she had wasted.

The problem is that there are no hard and fast rules about when to become exclusive. One prerequisite is to do so only if the other person also wants to become exclusive. The two of you should take at least three to six weeks to make this decision, as you will need the time to get to know each other. If this person is "the one," this period of time will only strengthen your relationship. Your potential mate will appreciate how much thought you give to important matters. And if it turns out this isn't the man or woman for you, you will have neither the agony of wasting four months with the wrong person nor the burden of beginning your plan again from scratch.

Of course, you must avoid the trap of constantly pushing people away because of your own fear of commitment and exclusivity. Keep your eye out for old patterns; be careful not to reject someone because he or she doesn't match your old list of what you want. If the person has many of the items on your master list, if you have been dating for a while, and if he or she wants to be exclusive with you, then it is probably a good idea to make this commitment. Still you should not abandon your plan like a hot potato. You may decide to stop running your classified ad, and to put your matchmaker on hold, but you should probably continue your volunteer work, your classes, and your sports club, just to keep in circulation. Getting asked out is a boost to your esteem even when you say no; if your relationship doesn't work out, you will know that you are still on track to getting married. Avoid locking yourself into an exclusive relationship that won't lead to marriage that you stay in simply because you have nothing to fall back on.

Remember, too, that when you feel momentum building in one area, you may become overconfident and forget about the other parts of your plan. As soon as you have three or four dates through the personal ads, you may decide to forget about joining a church. This would be a big mistake. Your objective is to leave no stone unturned! When the personal ads dry up for a little bit, your church dates will call you up. When that area is slow, your matchmaker will call. The more "out there" you are, the better your chances of finding "Mr. or Ms. Right"!

Step Three: Manage Your Busy Life

The third step is to work on being able to manage several areas of interest at the same time. By following your plan, your life will become incredibly full and busy. You might receive ten messages on your answering machine in one day! Your matchmaker has two new dates for you, the president of the volunteer organization wants to know if you can make it to dinner to meet someone special, you were accepted as a new member by the local business association, and you forgot to pick your dog up at the vet. Your key to having it all work is to return answering machine messages within twenty-four hours, and not say yes to everything that comes your way. Some people will be pleased to have so much activity in their lives, and others will just want to get the day over with. But the fact remains that *getting out there* is the single best strategy that you can devise to find a mate. So put up with it for a while, and when you are married, you and your loved one can hibernate all you want!

This chapter will assist you in implementing your plan by helping you determine where to look for information. The following guidelines cover all of the areas alluded to in Chapter 4. Apply all of this information to your individual list, and your to do list will likely grow as you go through this data. As discussed in the last chapter, networking is by far the best way to get introduced to your mate. This action step should be part of your daily activities. The other areas need to be looked at in detail.

Volunteering

There are many places to volunteer, and finding the right place for you will take a little research. But before you begin your research, keep in mind these general criteria before you become an active volunteer in a particular organization:

- Does the organization have activities that you are interested in?
- Does it have people in your age group participating?
- Does it have events where you are apt to run into a fairly steady stream of newcomers?
- Does it fit into your schedule?

Start your search by picking up your local paper and looking under the section "Volunteer Opportunities." It is likely that this column runs only once per week, so you may need to call the paper to find out on what day it runs. There are also lists published in city magazines, and for these, you need to visit the library to look them up. Ask the research librarian which magazines or newspapers are the best for finding this information.

The next step might be to phone a local community center. Many of these organizations are denominational, so that by volunteering in their organizations, you are likely to meet someone of the same religion or background. Community centers often have organized volunteer groups that throw annual events. So if working on events sounds like fun to you, a community center is a good place to find some action.

Some people like to do volunteer work that "makes a difference." Examples might include doing work for a cause, helping people in need, or working for an environmental group. There are probably areas that you have considered important, and thought that one day you might like to help out. Well, here's your opportunity. Calling up local or international agencies that are dedicated to your cause is the best way to find out what's available.

Friends are also an excellent source for finding your best volunteer situation. Find out where they have volunteered, or if they know of any organizations that could use a hand. You can also find out whether they know of volunteer groups that happen to have singles in your age group who volunteer there.

There are also specific community newspapers that have listings of volunteer groups, and advertisements for events that are coming up for charitable organizations. Attend some of these functions that are open to the public. While you are there, see what kind of people are running the event and what kind of people the organization attracts. Not only will you be donating your money to a worthy cause and meeting many people, but you may find a "home" with the organization.

Once you start looking for a volunteer organization, you will see that the town that you've come to think of as void of community activity is actually bustling with interested people getting out there. You should leave no stone unturned—join several volunteer organizations at once until you find the one that is right for you.

Personal Ads

Placing a personal ad is quite easy once you have written the ad. You may already have the right periodical in mind, or you may have to take a trip to the library to view all the local newspapers and magazines to make your selection. The questions that you should ask yourself before you place the ad are:

- Is this publication marketed to people like me?

- Do the other ads sound like people I would be interested in?

- Does the publication have a large enough or specific enough audience?

- Does the publication have box numbers available to ensure confidentiality?

Once you have found the publication or publications that you would like to place your ad in, get right to it. You want to start receiving your mail as soon as possible! Some of the publications might be quite costly, but if you want to get married, you've got to put your money where your mouth is. Besides, how much money have you wasted in the past on finding a mate? Now at least you have a plan, so this money is an investment. If it is easier financially for you to do things in stages, so be it. But do not let lack of money stand in your way, or mess up your plan for finding "Mr. or Ms. Right. '

Finding a Matchmaker

Finding a good matchmaker can be tricky. When a matchmaker answers the phone, he or she will tell you that he or she has the best list of potential dates in the country, that he or she has a "sixth sense" for finding the right person for you, and that if you sign up with this person, you will be married in less than a week. I wouldn't be too confident about all of this. But when you look in the local papers in the singles section, or in the phone book, there are many matchmakers and dating services to choose from, and all people or services will make similar claims. How do you choose the one that is right for you?

There are several questions that are important for you to ask yourself before selecting the best matchmaker for you:

- How long has this person or service been in business?
- How many members does this person or service have?
- What kind of clientele does this person or service attract?
- How personable is the matchmaker?
- Are the fees within my budget?
- How many dates does the service provide?
- How does the person or service handle confidentiality?
- Is the office convenient to my home or office?
- What is the matchmaker's track record?

Your next step is to go through the list of matchmakers and dating services, and interview each prospective candidate using the criteria previously listed. Keep accurate notes, and select the top three services to make personal appointments with. Keep in mind that even the matchmaker interviewing process is a valuable experience. They will ask you questions that will underscore many of the issues that we have been covering in terms of defining exactly what you are looking for, and in terms of being committed to getting married. You will likely sound like the ideal candidate to many people, given all of the work that you have already done—and you are. Many people that you will date will not be as determined as you, so don't get discouraged when you meet someone who is not as focused. It doesn't mean that person or dating service isn't "the one."

At the interview, ask to see information on, or pictures of, at least a few eligible clients. If there aren't at least three prospects that interest you, then the lead isn't worth pursuing. A matchmaker's lifeline is his or her ability to constantly attract new members. This is important for you so that you will meet as many new people as possible. Also, find out how persistent the matchmaker really is. Most fees are paid up front. Will this person keep you busy for a few weeks and then put your name at the bottom of the list? Will this person really work hard for you, or will you have to constantly be the one to chase after him or her for names? That may work, but given what we've already discussed, if you lose your enthusiasm for the project, a good matchmaker is an excellent fail-safe to keep you on target.

Also, don't judge a matchmaker by the fees. Yes, you can expect better service and a more select clientele with the higher fees charged by certain places. But don't let that stop you from joining a matchmaker with a little shop who does everything by jotting little notes to him- or herself on tiny scraps of paper. If this person has been in the business for twenty years, he or she is doing something right. And, if you are really determined, joining more than one matchmaker will increase your odds of meeting someone great. But there are only seven days in a week, and unless you are prepared to make breakfast, lunch, and dinner dates, one matchmaker should be sufficient to keep you busy along with all your other "getting out there" strategies.

Religious Sanctuaries

Finding out where there are appropriate churches or synagogues in your area is pretty straightforward. There are lists available at your town or city hall, in the phone book, and listings in newspapers, in magazines, at the library, and at local hotels. You can speak to friends or family members, or ask people at your place of work. It might also be valuable to get information on the religious institutions in the surrounding towns as well, just so that you are aware of all options available to you.

When you have a fairly thorough list compiled, ask yourself the following questions to narrow down your list:

- Is this denomination the one with which I grew up or with which I am comfortable?

- Is the church or synagogue close enough to where I live?

- Are there many people my age who attend services and events?

- Are there events there that are geared toward singles?

- Does the church or synagogue have active volunteer organizations?

- Does it have lectures and seminars?

- Does it have recreational activities in which members can participate?

- Is the clergyman someone with whom I feel comfortable?

- Are the people friendly and welcoming?

As in searching for a matchmaker, you will be able to narrow your list down to about three or four places by asking questions over the phone and taking extensive notes. Once this is done, be sure to visit each of the four top places when they are full of people. You will probably feel uncomfortable since you don't know anyone, but do your best to get the feel of the place, and see what kinds of people the congregants are. If you have the opportunity to talk to some people, by all means make the effort to do so. The long-standing members are the best sources of information. Pick up whatever newsletters and literature are available, and read the bulletin boards. Try not to be too judgmental, but after visiting four places, one of them will stick out in your mind as just feeling "right."

The Right Class
You are probably already aware of local places to take classes, but don't overlook the smaller organizations that attract many singles to them. First, start out by getting the course catalogs from as many institutions as you can. Your local library, Chamber of Commerce, or city hall will have listings of local schools and teaching organizations. Comb local newspapers for ads for schools or specific classes. Keep yours eyes and ears open to classes that other people are taking. Don't overlook these organizations: community colleges, universities, private colleges, night classes at high schools, the local YMCA, churches and synagogues, private institutions, community centers, and even group lessons in private homes.

Then, pick a few classes on which to follow up. Match each

class to your interests and time schedule, and go to a few to try them out. This is often allowed, and is a good way to see whether the crowd is what you're looking for or not, and if the topic is what you thought it was. When you do enroll in a course, take it seriously. Don't skip out when you simply "don't feel like going." Just as you are looking for a stable person, you don't know who is on the other side of the classroom watching to see how committed a person you are. Also, a class provides a nice routine in your life. It is very valuable not only during your searching process, but also for life in general. No matter what else is going on in the chaos of daily living, you force yourself to take time out to expand your mind on a regular basis. This is very healthy.

Business Associations

There are many business associations available, and they love to find new active members. If you are a professional, or have a very specific job title, you are probably inundated with literature from professional associations. There are seminars, lectures, and conferences, many of which are expensive, and conducted during business hours. But for your professional advancement, and especially to forward your goal of getting married, these events can be great if you choose wisely which to take advantage of. If you don't have time to sift through all the different opportunities, try to select events and associations that have recognizable names, or are presenting big speakers. The smaller organizations sometimes have very interesting agendas, and if one appeals to you, that's terrific, because you will meet people at that event who are also interested in that topic.

If you aren't inundated with association mail, a good place to start looking for these types of associations is in the journals that are geared toward your profession. If you don't know what these are, locate them in your library. Look at several past copies to see what kinds of associations exist, and what kinds of events they have sponsored. There are also organizations that aren't geared toward any specific profession, often called something like "The Downtown Business Association." These organizations may be the best places to meet people you don't already know, and you can find out about them by phoning the Chamber of Commerce. Other good sources for association information are the smaller, local newspapers which may have ads for various business events. You might even like an organization well enough to become a part of the governing body, or to help out as a volunteer. The key is to keep active by frequenting these types of events in order to meet as many people as possible.

Sports Clubs

Joining a sports club or other activity-oriented organization requires a bit of research. For a sports club, your options will probably be whatever is nearest your home or office. Where you join will depend on what kinds of activities you are interested in, if the sports club is co-ed, how many members it has, and whether you like the facilities or not. This is largely a matter of personal taste, and again, much of this information can be gathered over the telephone before you visit a few places. An especially valuable technique for choosing a sports club is to get people's opinions of the club. Often word of mouth is very valuable to get the real scoop on a place.

For other activity-oriented organizations, the best place to start is the library. A research librarian can tell you if there are any newspapers or magazines for your area that are specifically targeted to your particular area of interest. If so, they will have a wealth of information in them. Other places to look are in your local Sunday newspaper, in the "lifestyle" section. Look in national guides for local organizations, or local chapters of larger organizations. You can contact your local tourist bureau to see what's available, and you can also go to areas where your activity is practiced to meet other people who can give you advice on how to get involved.

The information listed in this chapter is not the only way to meet your mate. Be creative! Talk to a lot of people and find out where they met their mates, and then design a plan of action to emulate their methods. Then determine the best course of action to accomplish this. Remember, *you* are in control of your future! With determination, and implementing your plan step-by-step, you should be hearing wedding bells soon!

NOTEBOOK

1. Add more specific items to your to do lists from Chapter 4, using the information from this chapter.

2. Possible places to volunteer:

_____
Name of organization

_____   _____
Contact name   Phone #

_____
Information

_____

_____

_____

_____
Name of organization

_____   _____
Contact name   Phone #

_____
Information

_____

_____

_____

_____
Name of organization

_____   _____
Contact name   Phone #

_____
Information

_____

_____

_____

Name of organization

Contact name   Phone #

Information

_____

_____

_____

3. Possible publications in which to put personal ads:

Name of organization

Contact name   Phone #

Rates

Information

_____

_____

_____

Name of organization

Contact name   Phone #

Rates

Information

_____

_____

_____

Name of organization
_____

Contact name _____   Phone # _____

Rates _____

Information _____

_____

_____

_____

Name of organization
_____

Contact name _____   Phone # _____

Rates _____

Information _____

_____

_____

_____

Name of organization
_____

Contact name _____   Phone # _____

Rates _____

Information _____

_____

_____

_____

4. Possible matchmakers with whom to sign up:

Name of organization

Contact name   Phone #

Years in business   # of members

Rates   Interview this person? (yes/no)

Information

Name of organization

Contact name   Phone #

Years in business   # of members

Rates   Interview this person? (yes/no)

Information

Name of organization

Contact name   Phone #

Years in business   # of members

Rates   Interview this person? (yes/no)

Information

Name of organization

Contact name

Phone #

Years in business

# of members

Rates

Interview this person? (yes/no)

Information

_____

_____

Name of organization

Contact name

Phone #

Years in business

# of members

Rates

Interview this person? (yes/no)

Information

_____

_____

5. Possible churches or synagogues to attend:

Name of organization

Contact name

Phone #

Address/location

Denomination

Visit this sanctuary? (yes/no)

Information

_____

_____

Name of organization

Contact name   Phone #

Address/location

Denomination   Visit this sanctuary? (yes/no)

Information

Name of organization

Contact name   Phone #

Address/location

Denomination   Visit this sanctuary? (yes/no)

Information

Name of organization

Contact name   Phone #

Address/location

Denomination   Visit this sanctuary? (yes/no)

Information

Name of organization
_____

Contact name   Phone #
_____

Address/location
_____

Denomination   Visit this sanctuary? (yes/no)
_____

Information
_____

_____

_____

6. Possible classes to take:

Name of organization
_____

Contact name   Phone #
_____

Class information
_____

_____

_____

Name of organization
_____

Contact name   Phone #
_____

Class information
_____

_____

_____

Name of organization

Contact name   Phone #

Class information

_____

_____

Name of organization

Contact name   Phone #

Class information

_____

_____

Name of organization

Contact name   Phone #

Class information

_____

_____

7. Possible business associations in which to become active:

Name of organization

Contact name   Phone #

Information

_____

_____

Name of organization
_____

Contact name _____   Phone # _____

Information
_____
_____
_____

Name of organization
_____

Contact name _____   Phone # _____

Information
_____
_____
_____

Name of organization
_____

Contact name _____   Phone # _____

Information
_____
_____
_____

Name of organization
_____

Contact name _____   Phone # _____

Information
_____
_____
_____

8. Possible sports clubs or activity-oriented organizations in which to become active:

Name of organization
_____

Contact name _____   Phone # _____

Information _____

_____

_____

_____

_____

Name of organization
_____

Contact name _____   Phone # _____

Information _____

_____

_____

_____

_____

Name of organization
_____

Contact name _____   Phone # _____

Information _____

_____

_____

_____

_____

Name of organization
_____

Contact name   Phone #
_____

Information
_____

_____

_____

_____

Name of organization
_____

Contact name   Phone #
_____

Information
_____

_____

_____

_____

6

Those Horrible First Dates

DID YOU EVER notice that there is a unanimous hatred of first dates? It seems as if there is a conspiracy designed to undermine the most important and valuable way to discern whether a particular person is right for you or not. It is entirely understandable. First dates are very uncomfortable, tedious, and leave little room for being yourself. But, going on first dates and making them productive is a vital part of your mission.

The main point of getting out there is to meet as many people as possible so that you can go on as many first dates as possible. It is also advisable to spend at least a few hours on each date so that you really get to know the person. This is where the real meeting of the minds takes place, and the better you are at playing detective on these dates, the more efficient your project of finding the right mate will be.

There is specific information to find out, and specific character traits to look for in your date. These are outlined in this chapter. If you need to, write down what to look for on an index card, and carry it with you. Excuse yourself to the restroom to review these elements so that you make sure to find out about each of these areas before the date is over.

It is socially acceptable to talk about each other's life histories, and a lot of information can be garnered from this, but you need to develop the art of digging deeper. You can even start out the date (after you have ordered your food!) by saying that you want to make as much use of this time as possible to find out about him or her. People who are as determined as you to get married will find your direct approach refreshing. The kinds of people who would rather fritter away the hours with small talk, and depend on "chemistry" to see if they are good together, are not the kinds of people you want to be with anyway. So don't be shy, and get to work! Your mate may be the very next date you go on!

Gathering Information

These are the five items of information that you must find out about your date in the course of your discussions:

1. *What is most important to your date?* What does your date talk about the most? Does your date spend a half hour telling you about his or her new car? Does your date talk about his or her dog? Does your date talk about the importance of a balanced life? What kinds of activities does he or she spend time doing? And does what this person says is important to him or her correspond to what he or she does with his or her time?

   I once went on a date, and the man spent the entire evening telling me the story of his rise to power in his company. Not only did he reveal his finesse at stepping on people without them even knowing, but he made it absolutely clear that his success in business was what was most important to him. When I asked him about what kind of family life he wanted, the question caught him by surprise, almost as if he'd never given it any thought before. Just a few choice questions made it very clear to me that he did not match the items on my list.

2. *What is this person's family life like?* How does your date get along with his or her parents, siblings, extended family? This is very telling as to what this person will be like as a mate. He or she may have had a bad family life, but depending on whether he or she has a "sour grapes" attitude or a "let's make the best of it" attitude can make a world of difference to your future with this person. Someone who is genuine in the commitment and determination to create a wonderful family life is worth his or her weight in gold. Be very thorough in your inquiries about this subject and on discerning what kind of future family life you think that this person wants.

Audrey had been married for four years to a very nice man named Donald. But they had many problems in their marriage because she desperately wanted children and he didn't. If you can believe it, they had never discussed the subject before they got married!

After two years of marriage, Audrey started to bring the subject up, and she was horrified to learn how Donald felt. She was also very angry that he had never told her that he didn't want kids. His response was that at the time they got married, he wavered on the subject, so he couldn't have given her a definitive answer then. But now he said that he was certain that he didn't want the financial and psychological burden of raising a family.

Audrey was devastated. If they had discussed this before they were married, at least she would have had a choice, and maybe at that time she and Donald could have made a decision together to only have one or two children. They would have been compromising together instead of getting themselves into a very painful and difficult situation.

I really don't know how they will work this out, but one thing is for sure, they had a lot more choices before they got married than they do now. That is why it is so important for you to have these conversations with dates long before the subject of marriage ever comes up.

3. *How well does your date match the items on your master list?* You should know your list by heart. Don't hesitate to ask questions about your date's values. What is more important to this person: social, spiritual, or intellectual pursuits? Some of the items you are looking for you will be able to recognize right away, like politeness or a sense of humor. Other traits, such as honesty or patience, may take longer to discern. Figuring out how many items your date matches will help you to determine if your date is "the one" for you.

4. *What is this person searching for in a mate?* This is a very important, and often overlooked, question, which is vital in terms of your future with this person. Not only is it a little bit tricky to find this out tactfully, but your date may not even know the answer to the question. Or, this person may give you an answer that he or she thinks you want to hear. But,

nonetheless, pursuing the answer to this question will not only assist you in learning more about your prospective partner, it will be very valuable for your search.

I once dated a man who didn't match any of the items on my list, and I was also totally unsuited for him as well. But because he had no idea what he was looking for in a mate, he kept pursuing me. Finally, on the phone, I told him that he was not what I was looking for, and that if he made a list of the top ten things he wanted in a woman, he would see clearly that I also was not suited for him. It was a very amusing phone call, and he was stunned by how straightforward I was. But after he hung up, I really think he was going to make a list for himself.

5. *What is this person's vision for the future?* Get basic outlines, not necessarily specifics. It's better to find out now that your date is planning a two-year trip to Tibet than after you have been dating for six months. Also listen very carefully to what your date says. If this person says that children are important to him or her yet this person has five kids from a previous marriage that he or she visits every second year, you know you can't be so sure about what this person says. Finally, once your date tells you what his or her vision is, find out what steps this person is taking to realize his or her goals.

Many people don't have visions or pictures in their minds as to where they want to be in the future. They are waiting to see what life is going to hand them. Or, in many cases, they have given up on their dreams, having been beaten down by the realities of daily living. But, if you ask someone what his or her vision is and give this person a little encouragement, he or she may open up and talk about dreams of how life could really be.

Ted, who worked at a car dealership, always had the vision of becoming a famous actor. He found dating very frustrating because women always rolled their eyes at him, and never took his dreams seriously. I told him that while I respected his vision for the future, I could see why women reacted that way. Many women who are looking for a mate are looking for stability, and acting careers don't have the best track record. I suggested that he either find a woman who was willing to stick out the years of uncertainty with him, or to alter his vision a little bit. Maybe he could focus all his attention at being successful at the car dealership, and have his acting as a hobby.

To find someone that complemented his dreams, Ted would have to search for a while, but if he wanted to be a famous actor so much, the wait would be worth it. The point is that you want to find a mate whose life vision is either similar to yours, or that is complementary, so that you can each support the other in your respective visions.

Discovering Character Traits

The following are the five character traits that you must find out about your date in the course of your discussions:

1. *What is your date's attitude about life?* Is it compatible with yours? Does this person seem resigned that nothing will ever go as planned? Does this person put everyone and everything down? (Guess who's next?) Is this person closed-minded about certain ideas without thinking the ideas through first? Is your date totally caught up in the past and angry that life hasn't dedicated itself to making him or her happy? Or, is enthusiasm a key trait? Do you feel encouraged to tell your story? Does this person praise things that you say? Is your date interested in learning about new things?

   I once went to dinner at the home of a married couple who had opposing attitudes about life. Every time he made a derogatory remark, she would put it in a more positive light. And when she said something uplifting, he would point out a negative side to her statement. It seemed to work for them, but it was difficult to sit through for three hours. I don't think necessarily that having the opposite attitude is bad, but I guess this couple's way of handling it just didn't seem to be compatible. They seemed to be confronting one another all the time. Compatibility in attitude is so important because, no matter how much you think you can, you truly cannot change someone's overall attitude about life. You had better like it, or you could be unhappy for a very long time!

2. *Does your date listen?* Does your date ask you about what's important to you, or seem to care about what you are say-

ing? Does your date ask you to clarify things he or she doesn't completely understand, and ask you your opinions about things? Or is this person enraptured with the sound of his or her own voice? Does your date ask you the same questions over again? Does this person talk to you while gazing around the room? Do you get the feeling your date isn't even there? Be certain that you are with someone who listens to you. You may have a pattern of finding people who ignore you, but you must break this pattern. You deserve to be listened to! What's the point of finding a mate if you're going to be alone anyway?

Also, remember that there is superficial listening and genuine listening. My friend Julia was dating a man for a while, and he seemed to really care about what she said and what was going on with her. It was only when she was in the crisis situation of losing her job that she discovered that he only listened when he wanted to. Julia was very frightened about her job situation, and he was not there to support her. She felt like he only listened to her when it was convenient for him, and when he didn't have to feel uncomfortable or intimate. She was very glad to discover this before she got any closer to him. She recognized that what she needed in a mate was someone who really listened to her and was there when she needed him.

3. *How thoughtful and caring is this person?* Does your date let a door slam in your face? Does this person shout rudely at the waiter? Grab the bread first? Or, does your date ask you if you like the menu? Is this person considerate enough to reach over to help you clean up a spill? These subtle actions let you know that this person is thinking about your welfare. On a first date, lack of these qualities may be a sign that this person just never learned how to be thoughtful. It is possible to learn later in life, but not probable. If your date does show thoughtfulness on a first date, it is not a definitive sign that this person is wonderful. People can pretend to be thoughtful, but sooner or later they won't be able to keep up the facade, and you will see a marked change in their behavior. Keep your eyes open for this quality, as thoughtfulness is very important in a strong relationship.

4. *How much acting does your date do?* Is there a particular facade that this person has developed over decades of practice that is impossible to penetrate? Do you find yourself coming up against one "line" after another? Do you find it difficult to be yourself? Or, does this person laugh at his or her own foibles? Is your date sincere in his or her attempts to find out what you're really like? Does your date answer your questions honestly, not just saying what you want to hear? Don't expect to get to know someone intimately on the first date; it does take time to wear down people's natural walls so they can actually just "be." A little bit of a facade is natural on a first date, but spending the whole evening trying to impress each other may be a sign that the two of you don't bring out the best in each other.

5. *How committed is this person?* Does this person have a long history of changed jobs and changed relationships? Has your date moved twenty-five times in the last three years? Does this person say one thing and do another? Keep promises to people? Meet you at the scheduled time? Does this person take commitments very seriously? Does he or she have a history of long-standing commitments? Has this person had one sustained area of interest for ten years? Does he or she have a full appointment book and keep appointments? Have a dedicated hobby or sport?

   Someone who is serious and committed is a good candidate for making a commitment to marriage and to a solid, stable relationship. Look for consistency in their interests and their behavior. Beware of people who float from one interest to another, posing as eccentric when in reality they have no idea what it means to stick things out, especially when the going gets rough. This quality may take some time to assess, but even on the first date, it is still possible to discern approximately how committed a person is.

   Suzette was so impressed with a diplomat that she was dating because he had lived all over the world and spoke four languages. He had held many fascinating government posts, and was part of the Washington social circles that she had always dreamed about. She told me that she felt sorry for him because, although he had been in a great number of relationships, he had said that no one could ever really understand the pressures of his position. He had never been able to find the right woman to settle down with. He also boasted to her that he had the luxury and clout of moving to another country if he found himself in a difficult situation.

On the surface, these comments seem innocuous enough, but if you look behind someone's smooth veneer to see how really committed he or she is, certain facts come to the surface. For instance, how committed to finding the right woman to settle down with must this man have been if he was willing to blame his entire failure to do so on his dates' lack of understanding of the pressures of his position? And eliciting sympathy from Suzette is obviously the perfect ploy to get close to her, but not for the intention of creating a healthy, stable relationship. Also, this man boasts that he very conveniently set his life up so that he can bolt at the first sign of difficulty! How well does that bode for a relationship with him? I am not saying to tear someone apart, I am suggesting to really listen to what is behind what someone says. Trying to find out what someone is committed to is one good way to really learn about him.

Revealing Your Story

In the normal course of conversation, the same information that you are looking to find out about your date will be disclosed about you. Your date will learn what is most important to you, about your family life, about what you're searching for, and about your vision for the future. When these areas are in sync between the two of you, you will have something far more potent and valuable than chemistry. You will have the foundation to build a very healthy and stable relationship, the kind that will grow into a good solid marriage!

And, your date is also learning about your character traits at the same time you are studying his or hers. Your date will learn about your attitudes, how well you listen, how thoughtful you are, how much of an actor you are, and how committed you are. This certainly puts you on the spot, too, and may make some people a bit uncomfortable. But it is very important for both of you to see these traits in each other. There are many people out there who aspire to marry others with all the fine qualities, but they have not mastered those qualities themselves.

In the first several chapters of this book, you have learned many things about yourself, and have come a long way toward designing yourself to be the other half of a great team. But when you read the last section on character traits, did you recognize yourself? Could you see areas for improvement? Go through the section again, and jot down in your notebook character traits that you could work on, and specific actions you could take to improve your ability to marry someone of true quality.

There are also a few things to keep in mind on first dates that will make the dating process a little bit easier.

1. *Memorize your life story.* Get the concise, interesting story down to five enthusiastic minutes or less. Instead of wasting valuable time telling the same boring story (and getting sick of hearing your own voice), you can concentrate on listening to who your date is, and on discussing all of the aforementioned topics!

2. *Don't be a chameleon.* Just because your date is a baseball fan doesn't mean you need to pretend you are. Be yourself! If you keep changing to suit whomever you are with, how will the right person recognize you when he or she sees you?

3. *Don't prejudge a candidate.* How many times have you heard couples who have been married for thirty years say, "When I first met Joe, I couldn't stand him!" Or, "We knew each other for two years, but we had just never thought of each other in that way." The right guy might be lurking behind the wrong body type. Or the perfect woman might make a poor first impression, but would make the most loving wife. Don't judge so quickly that you miss your chance when it's right in front of you! Spend the time to get to know what a person is really like.

4. *Rejection is part of the game.* Don't be so surprised every time it happens. Expect it! Face it, out of the one hundred plus dates it may take to find "Mr. or Ms. Right," ninety-nine are not right for you! That's ninety-nine failed attempts. Some of those you'll reject, and some will reject you. Don't make it a habit to reject everyone right away to preempt a person from rejecting you. Learn to handle rejection, sulk, do what you must, but then get right back to work on your master plan!

5. *Keep working on your character traits.* There is nothing quite as attractive as someone who is strong enough to work on him- or herself. (There is a big difference between working on yourself because you think that there is something wrong with you, and working on yourself because you want to be the best you that you can be!) Talk to people who have the kind of qualities you want, and emulate them. Choose role models who typify those traits. Take an etiquette class, read self-help books, work on one character trait at a time. And don't be hard on yourself! Look at this as a fun project, and have fun doing it! You don't need to be perfect to find someone, but working on your character traits is always valuable, even after you are married.

6. *Do not be "intimate."* Yes, this means what you think it does. Being a member of a society that is addicted to immediate gratification, and the "pseudo" intimacy that comes from physical contact, you may find this to be a difficult constraint. But building a strong relationship takes strength of character. This act of restraint is possibly the single greatest statement you can make to your date that you are of great value and don't give yourself away to just anybody. Physical intimacy should be the last, not the first, of the intimacies that you establish in a relationship. In terms of building a stable relationship, this is very important. Refer to Chapter 8 for more information on this subject.

7. *Do not talk about any of your old relationships.* Even if your date asks. Do not give details or names, or *ever* make any comparisons between your date and an old boyfriend or girlfriend. This is true for the first date, and holds true for one hundred years of marriage! Your past is yours! There is not one thing you can say that is harmless. Every word is like a dagger, *even* if you use the information to help someone learn more about you. Try to think of a way to tell your date this information without referring back to a relationship.

8. *Complete every date completely.* You just spent a great deal of time and effort ridding yourself of "dangling relationships," why create a whole slew of them now? When a date is nearing the end, if you do not want to see the person

again, simply say that you have had a very nice evening, but that you don't think that the two of you have enough in common. And leave it at that. If your date protests, just keep repeating that line over and over again until the person gets it. If you *do* want to see the person again, say that you had a very enjoyable time, and you would like to see the person again. If your date agrees, set up a time. If your date doesn't, he or she probably won't say so. Your date will probably say, "I'll be in touch." Thus the old waiting game begins, and a future "dangling relationship" is born.

Do not let this happen to you. Complete every date completely, if not verbally, then in your mind. If a person doesn't agree on a new time to meet, you can call once or twice to follow up (he or she sincerely might need to check their calendar, or may be going out of town), but in your mind, consider it over. You cannot afford the mental time that waiting around and hoping cost you. You have a mate to find, and the more dates you go on, the better your chances! And wouldn't you be the picture of strength if that last date who finally got his or her act together to call you invited you out and you already were booked for the next three weekends!

NOTEBOOK

1. Make a list of every reason you can possibly think of as to why you hate first dates:

_____

_____

_____

_____

_____

_____

_____

_____

_____

_____

2. Make a list of what valuable information can be learned about someone on a first date:

_____

_____

_____

_____

_____

_____

3. Make an index card to carry with you listing the five items of information to find out about your date. Make an index card to carry with you listing the five character traits to find out about your date.

4. In reviewing the section on character traits, which areas could you work on to make yourself a better mate?

_____

_____

_____

_____

_____

_____

_____

_____

5. Practice telling your life story to a friend, keeping it under five minutes. (Clock yourself!) Write down any phrases that will help you remember important points.

_____

_____

_____

_____

_____

_____

_____

_____

_____

_____

_____

_____

_____

6. Review your list of what you are looking for in a mate (from Chapter 3) and add any character traits that are important to you. (You must maintain only ten items on the list, so cross off other items if you need to.)

_____

_____

_____

_____

_____

_____

_____

_____

_____

_____

_____

_____

_____

7

Managing Your Progress

THIS CHAPTER MIGHT be the most important chapter in the entire book. You have come a long way since page one. You have taken a good look at yourself, prepared your environment, designed an incredible list of what you are looking for in a mate, made a plan to accomplish your mission, started to implement this plan, and even begun going out on dates. You have done a lot of work, and should not only be very proud of what you have accomplished so far, but you should also feel a certain sense of control over your future that you may not be used to feeling.

It is time now to step back from all the bustle of activity you've been creating, and look at how far you've come, where you are now, and where you are going. You know now more than ever before, that *you have the power over your own future*. Whether you have followed all the directions in this book or not, you can see clearly that *results* come from *commitments* and *actions*. And *you* have the power to make commitments and to perform actions. There is no big secret to getting exactly what you are committed to getting. Just do the appropriate actions to get it. But if it were that simple, you'd already be married. It is what stands in your way of making commitments and performing actions that must be overcome before you can get what you want.

Jessica told me that she really liked many of the ideas in the book, but she had decided that she just was not ready to commit to marriage yet. She had followed along in each chapter, and had done much of the notebook work, but had not followed the plan she had made, and had not gone on any dates.

This news obviously concerned me. I felt that my job was to find out what obstacle was standing in Jessica's way, and to do whatever I could to assist her in removing it. We talked on the phone for hours. She told me some of her dating history, and a lot about her early family life, but nothing she said seemed to be standing in her way. She mentioned that she was having a hard time getting past the Hollywood image that she had always wanted in a man, but it seemed to me that she was working hard on this. Jessica and I just could not figure out what was in her way.

And then about a week later, I came across an article in a magazine about superachievers in the business world. As I read each biography, it seemed that they all had one thing in common. When each person achieved a big goal, there was one fabulous moment of glory, followed by a sense of emptiness, a feeling of "Is that all there is?" I had a feeling that this was what was holding Jessica back from moving forward with her plan.

When I spoke to her about this, she acknowledged that it was not fear of failure, but rather fear of success that was probably stopping her. She knew that if she really set her mind to following her plan, she would be engaged within six months. Not only was this thought unnerving, but she was actually afraid to find "Mr. Right" because she knew that he could never match her expectations. Her fantasies were so much nicer than reality.

High expectations (and the feeling that once you find "the one" your whole life will be perfect), is very common. People are often disappointed that having great relationships doesn't protect them from the risks of everyday life. There is no such thing as escaping into "marital bliss!" The answer to the question, is that all there is? is yes! Life will still have its ups and downs. Problems and conflicts will still get in the way. The realities of life will not disappear.

Recognition was Jessica's first step toward getting on the other side of this obstacle. It will probably take her a little while to get over the loss of the "happily ever after" fantasy that she always thought she'd find someday. This process of discovering your obstacles, and creating ways to overcome them, is what will assist you in getting where you want to go.

This chapter will get down to the nitty gritty of what it's really going to take for you to get married. It is time to cut in deeper than you previously dared. You are going to need to be brutally honest with yourself. It will take an in-depth self-examination in order to complete the notebook section of this chapter.

This is the time to stop using the same excuses of why you're not married, and *make it happen*. Even if you are barrelling along on your project, you also need to have a breakthrough to produce the results to which you are committed.

Christopher was pursuing his plan with a vengeance, but he still had several "dangling relationships" he was clinging to. He had one old girlfriend that he called after every date to discuss all the details. Christopher had a condescending attitude to begin with, but with this woman's help, he would verbally tear each date apart, laughing hysterically at the date's foibles. Nothing I said to him could convince him that this was a big obstacle in his way.

The purpose of this chapter is to try to assist you to identify the obstacles that are in your way, and to help you get around or through them. So far in this book there have been chapters followed by the notebook work. In this chapter, the notebook is the major portion of the chapter. Take your time on the notebook work. Put check marks next to the items on which you intend to follow up. Even if this chapter takes you a week or a month to finish, it's okay; it is an extremely valuable process. Be very thorough and candid in your answers.

NOTEBOOK

From Chapter 1: EMOTIONAL PREPARATION

1. What difficulties have you had in keeping your commitment to get married?

_____

_____

_____

_____

_____

_____

2. What obstacles or incidents keep occurring that make you want to give up on your commitment to get married?

_____

_____

_____

_____

_____

_____

3. What have you done to get yourself back on track in your commitment to get married?

_____

_____

_____

_____

_____

_____

4. What kind of support system have you created to support your commitment to get married?

_____

_____

_____

_____

_____

_____

_____

5. What issues still persist from the past that get in the way of your pursuing a stable relationship?

_____

_____

_____

_____

_____

_____

_____

6. What patterns keep reoccurring from the past that get in your way of relating to people?

_____

_____

_____

_____

_____

_____

7. What issues from the past do you continue to bury under the rug, hoping they will go away by themselves?

_____

_____

_____

_____

_____

_____

8. Are you still holding onto a bad relationship that is neither healthy nor stable, but that fits all of your old patterns?

_____

9. What have you done to create new role models for yourself?

_____

_____

_____

_____

_____

_____

10. What have you done to study the elements that make up a healthy, stable relationship?

_____

_____

_____

_____

_____

_____

11. What areas can you see that you haven't been willing to work on, that you would be willing to work on now?

_____

_____

_____

_____

_____

_____

From Chapter 2: ENVIRONMENTAL PREPARATION

1. Do your living quarters still scream out, "Single person lives here"? What resistance do you have to preparing yourself to be married?

_____

_____

_____

_____

_____

_____

2. Do you still hold onto any photographs of old relationships? What attachment do you still have to the people in the picture? When do you plan to let go of them?

_____

_____

_____

_____

_____

_____

3. What mementos are you still holding onto? What do they mean to you? What is standing in your way of getting rid of them?

_____

_____

_____

_____

_____

_____

4. What gifts do you still cling to? Have you thoroughly convinced yourself that they have nothing to do with the person who gave them to you? Do you resent having to get rid of them? What would it take for you to get rid of them?

_____

_____

_____

_____

_____

_____

5. Do you still have old "dangling relationships" cluttering up your life? What is your resistance to eliminating them?

_____

_____

_____

_____

_____

_____

6. What difficulty have you had calling these people, speaking to them, and completing this project?

_____

_____

_____

_____

_____

_____

_____

7. Can you pinpoint ways in which these old relationships stop you from moving forward in your life?

_____

_____

_____

_____

_____

_____

_____

8. What actions have you been unable to take, that you would be willing to commit to taking now?

_____

_____

_____

_____

_____

_____

_____

From Chapter 3: MAKING A LIST

1. What resistance do you have to making a list?

_____

_____

_____

_____

_____

_____

_____

2. What have you done to overcome this resistance?

_____

_____

_____

_____

_____

_____

_____

3. How have you been dismantling your ideals and your "pictures" of the ideal mate?

_____

_____

_____

_____

_____

_____

_____

4. What wants are you still unwilling to give up that might be the exact thing that is standing in your way of finding the person to marry? (Wants include "looks like a model," "must be rich," or "has to love tennis.")

_____

_____

_____

_____

_____

_____

_____

5. What resistance do you have to getting beyond materialism?

_____

_____

_____

_____

_____

_____

_____

6. How has materialism guided your search thus far?

_____

_____

_____

_____

_____

_____

_____

7. What was difficult about writing down who you want to be in five years?

_____

_____

_____

_____

_____

_____

_____

8. What did you discover about yourself that helped you decide what you were looking for in a mate?

_____

_____

_____

_____

_____

_____

_____

9. What was difficult about determining your values?

_____

_____

_____

_____

_____

_____

_____

10. Did you recognize any of the "false" meanings of life in your own values? Did recognizing them assist you to determine what was really important to you?

   _____

11. Was the section on ethics hard to read because you saw that maybe you didn't have as high ethical values as you thought? How have your ethics improved since then?

   _____

   _____

12. Did you find it just about impossible to narrow your list down to ten items? Do you carry around the whole list with you for fear that you might forget about a quality that is important to you?

   _____

13. Do you have difficulty making decisions? Are you willing to make a decision now, even if it is wrong, just to flex the muscle of decision making?

   _____

14. Do you find that you get confused between being critical of someone and being clear on what you are looking for? What do you intend to do about this in the future?

   _____

   _____

   _____

   _____

   _____

   _____

   _____

15. What stands in your way of being determined and persistent?

_____

_____

_____

_____

_____

_____

16. If you could have any quality that you feel would make your search more productive, what would that quality be?

_____

_____

17. Besides making the commitment to get that quality into your life, what actions can you take to do it?

_____

_____

_____

_____

_____

_____

18. What stops you from thinking that you deserve to have the best life possible? What are you willing to do to build your self-esteem so that you do feel that you deserve this?

_____

_____

_____

_____

_____

From Chapter 4: MAKING A PLAN

1. What resistance do you have to making a plan?

_____

_____

_____

_____

_____

_____

_____

2. What value did you find in making a plan?

_____

_____

_____

_____

_____

_____

_____

3. What resistance do you have to controlling your own future?

_____

_____

_____

_____

_____

_____

_____

4. What short-term goals keep you from moving forward in your mission?

_____

_____

_____

_____

_____

_____

_____

5. What has been stopping you from planning for the long run? What fears do you have about the future?

_____

_____

_____

_____

_____

_____

_____

6. What resistance do you have to getting out there?

_____

_____

_____

_____

_____

_____

7. What stops you from telling people that you are looking to get married?

_____

_____

_____

_____

_____

_____

_____

8. What resistance do you have to volunteer work?

_____

_____

_____

_____

_____

_____

_____

9. If you haven't done so, what stops you from placing a personal ad?

_____

_____

_____

_____

_____

_____

_____

10. What stops you from going to a matchmaker?

_____

_____

_____

_____

_____

_____

_____

11. What stops you from joining a church or synagogue?

_____

_____

_____

_____

_____

_____

_____

12. What stands in your way of taking classes?

_____

_____

_____

_____

_____

_____

_____

13. What stops you from participating in business organizations?

_____

_____

_____

_____

_____

_____

14. What stops you from joining a sports club or other activity-oriented club?

_____

_____

_____

_____

_____

_____

15. Have you had difficulty prioritizing your plan?

_____

16. What is standing in your way of creating a to do list for each item on your list?

_____

_____

_____

_____

_____

_____

17. What have you been unwilling to do, that you could commit yourself to doing now?

_____

_____

_____

_____

_____

_____

_____

From Chapter 5: IMPLEMENTATION

1. What obstacles stand in your way of implementing your plan?

_____

_____

_____

_____

_____

_____

_____

2. What have you been putting off doing?

_____

_____

_____

_____

_____

_____

3. On which areas did you give up because you didn't achieve the immediate results that you wanted?

_____

_____

_____

_____

_____

_____

_____

4. What areas have you pursued that have been successful for you (volunteering, personal ads, matchmaker, church or temple, classes, business associations, sports clubs, or activity-oriented organizations)?

_____

_____

_____

_____

_____

_____

5. Did you have a difficult time getting started on your plan?

_____

6. What slowed the momentum of your plan? Failure or success?

_____

7. How difficult is it for you to manage several areas of interest at the same time?

_____

_____

8. What have you been unwilling to implement, that you could commit yourself to implementing now?

_____

_____

_____

_____

_____

_____

_____

From Chapter 6: THOSE HORRIBLE FIRST DATES

1. How do you feel about first dates?

_____

_____

_____

_____

_____

_____

_____

2. How has your dislike and fear of first dates interfered with your ability to accomplish your mission?

_____

_____

_____

_____

_____

_____

3. What stops you from finding out the *information* on a first date (what's important to your date, family life, matching your list, what your date is searching for, your date's vision)?

_____

_____

_____

_____

_____

_____

_____

4. How does "seeing what you want to see" stop you from really examining people's *character traits*?

_____

_____

_____

_____

_____

_____

5. Which character traits do you find hardest to discover in your date (attitude, listening skills, thoughtfulness, phoniness, commitments)?

_____

_____

_____

_____

_____

_____

_____

6. Which character traits did you identify within yourself that you would like to work on?

_____

_____

_____

_____

_____

_____

_____

7. What have you done to work on these traits?

_____

_____

_____

_____

_____

_____

_____

8. What is your biggest hurdle in becoming the kind of person another person of quality would want to marry? What do you intend to do about this?

_____

_____

_____

_____

_____

_____

_____

9. Do you still find yourself being a chameleon on dates? What do you intend to do about this?

_____

_____

_____

_____

_____

_____

_____

10. What is your reaction when someone rejects you?

_____

_____

_____

_____

_____

_____

11. How do you handle this rejection?

_____

_____

_____

_____

_____

_____

12. What might you do in the future that might be more productive?

_____

_____

_____

_____

_____

_____

_____

13. Is it difficult for you to refrain from being "intimate"? What patterns persist that keep you doing the same thing over and over again? What do you intend to do about it?

_____

_____

_____

_____

_____

_____

_____

14. What stops you from completing every date completely?

_____

_____

_____

_____

_____

_____

_____

15. Have you racked up a lot more dangling relationships? What do you intend to do about them?

_____

_____

_____

_____

_____

_____

_____

16. How has going on first dates assisted you in getting a clearer picture of what you are looking for in a mate?

_____

_____

_____

_____

_____

_____

17. What change in attitude have you been unwilling to make that you would be willing to change now?

_____

_____

_____

_____

_____

_____

18. What have you been unwilling to do, that you could commit to doing now with regard to *getting out there* more?

_____

_____

_____

_____

_____

_____

Continue Managing Your Progress

Congratulations! You have now completed a massive amount of work! By going through this process, you will have a better understanding of what it's really going to take for you to get married.

Scott called me for advice. He said that he was going through the book very steadily, until he got to the section on character traits. As I found out in our discussion, he saw certain traits in himself that he just couldn't bear to look at. In the section on attitude, he realized that he was a terrible listener, more concerned about what people thought of him than anything they had to say. He also didn't feel that he was a very committed person.

This would stop many people from going forward. But what I explained to Scott is that, first of all, his ability to see his weaknesses and acknowledge them is the primary step to developing better character traits. Once he is aware of these things, and is committed to changing them, his actions will start to correlate with how he wants to be. He will start to listen better and be more thoughtful. And, he should also get role models and read about ways to improve in each specific area.

Secondly, I told Scott that he should forgive himself for not being perfect. Yes, it is nice to work on character traits, but he doesn't need to be "perfect" to find "Ms. Right." And by moving forward with his plan, he will give himself the necessary practice of working on his traits and developing his sense of self-acceptance.

The information garnered from this kind of work will lead you to take certain actions that you otherwise would not have taken. The process will also have an effect on your behavior, which you may not even be aware of or need to control. That is the power that comes from recognizing and acknowledging your weaknesses. The proof is that when you are in a situation where you previously would have acted one way, now, somehow, you manage to act in a more constructive and powerful way. You will see. Your old patterns are already loosening the grip they have on you. Keep your eyes open to witness these changes that are taking place within you. You deserve a lot of credit for them.

Managing the progress of your goals and following your plan is a hefty task. You are managing your emotional well-being, the logistics of your plan, and the process of self-growth that comes with this project. But designing your own future has rewards! You are creating yourself to be the other half of "Mr. or Ms. Right." You are developing strengths and qualities that are very valuable for when you are married. You are learning how to create a balanced life for yourself. This project has made you busier than you might ever have been!

What you must also remember in managing your progress is that resignation is a normal part of the process of trying to find someone to marry. For some reason, people don't expect resignation, and think that the job of finding people will be easy just because they are determined. People often become resigned to the fact that their searches are fruitless, and that their visions will never be fulfilled. This is what stops many people from moving on and getting married. Just keep in mind that setbacks often come right before big breakthroughs, that you are in this for the long haul, and that you will get what you are looking for!

Nicole called me up because she was so frustrated and resigned and was, in fact, totally sick of this project altogether! She started to tell me all of the reasons that she was going to give up her search, when call-waiting clicked in on her line. She got off the phone with me, but called me back five minutes later to say that a man she had given up on had come back into town and was taking her out on Saturday night!

I wouldn't count on outside circumstances to keep you committed and to keep resignation from coloring your attitude. But certainly sticking to your plan will increase the likelihood of getting picked up when you are down. Persistence will pay off! (By the way, Nicole should use her renewed enthusiasm to recommit to her plan. If she waits till Saturday night to "see how it goes," and it doesn't go well, then on Sunday morning she's going to be worse off than she is now. She should call her matchmaker right away to get set up on more dates, put another ad in the personal column, and call back several responses from her last ad.)

Another part of the process is that you must deal with loneliness. Coming home from a date with what seemed to be such a promising candidate, and then ending up by being rejected by someone you wouldn't even introduce to your worst enemy, are some of the hazards of your mission. Going to a movie or delving into a good novel are good ways to overcome this loneliness. But when things get rough, just keep sticking to your plan. You will be surprised at how elastic your mind is. Just stay on track, do not give up, and nothing will stand in the way of your commitment to getting married!

8

Developing a Stable Relationship

IF YOU'RE LIKE many people, the words stable and relationship are mutually exclusive! The purpose of this chapter is to learn about the four cornerstones of a stable relationship: communication, integrity, trust, and commitment. These key factors combine to create a solid foundation on which to build your relationship. They will be useful to you when you find someone who you really enjoy being with, and most importantly, someone who matches many items on your list. Rather than following old unhealthy patterns, these cornerstones give you a guide to build a stable relationship that will hopefully serve you through a lifetime of marriage.

Communication

Communication is expressed through listening, speaking, and actions. If someone sits you down to tell you something that is very important to him or her, and you don't listen fully, you are communicating to that person that you don't care. If you develop the art of listening to others in the way that you would want to be listened to, it will create a stable and comforting relationship. And being careful of what you say to people takes a lot of thoughtfulness and care. If you lash out in anger, those words will stick for a long time. And your actions also speak volumes about how you feel about someone. Following are these three facets of communication in greater detail.

Listening

Listening is the first part of communication. It cannot only be interpreted in terms of what you hear, but also in terms of how you perceive things. When you are listening to someone, you are at the same time judging that person. This is a very natural process, but it does get in the way of the ability to really hear what the person is trying to say. The more you remove your own opinions while you are listening, the more you can understand a person and learn about who this person is. This is not easy to do, and there are many books on the art of listening, but if you keep a few things in mind, you should be able to start practicing this skill.

The first thing to notice is when you are not listening. Notice when you are in the middle of a conversation with someone, and you keep interrupting that person. Notice when you are nodding your head in response to someone, when in reality you haven't heard a word that person has said!

One man that I dated took me to a sports bar, and sat me at a table with my back to a large screen television set. He then proceeded to simultaneously watch the basketball game, eat his dinner, drink a beer, and tell me his life story! Needless to say, as soon as we finished eating, I cordially made my exit.

Try your best to stop yourself from gazing around the room when someone is talking to you. Pay attention to times when you think to yourself, "I know what this person is going to say next." Try to avoid being defensive, and arguing every point. Even if you are "right," the other person still deserves to make his or her point. By noticing when you are not listening, you can gain more control of your listening, thereby strengthening your listening muscle.

One technique is to say to yourself, "Don't talk, listen!" Repeat these words to yourself over and over again even while you are with someone else. It will help you ask more questions, and be more attentive to what the other person is saying. Your goal is to have a thoroughly satisfying feeling of really having heard what was said. Get to know who this person really is.

I remember an experience which really drove this message home to me. I was going to lunch with a woman who wanted desperately to get married, and a mutual friend had put the two of us together. We sat down at the table, and having dealt with this situation so intensively, and feeling confident in my ability to help, I immediately launched into a great deal of information that I thought would be useful.

After about twenty minutes, she stopped me. She said that she wasn't sure how much our mutual friend had told me, but that she had been married before, and had been in the most wonderful relationship, but that her husband had died in a car accident. What this woman so politely pointed out to me was that I had not listened to who she was. I realized that the advice that I had been giving her did not pertain to her, and I apologized. I spent the next hour listening to her, and I was then able to truly assist her in her goal to get remarried.

Also, while you are listening to someone, examine your own desire to want the person to be who you *think* this person is, rather than who this person *really* is. Many people convince themselves that they know another person really well. How many times have you heard someone say, "Gee, I've only known you for two weeks, but I feel like I've known you all of my life?" This is a very nice sentiment, but that is all it is, a sentiment. A person will be shocked three weeks later when that person starts acting differently than he or she expected. It is a recipe for disaster. Listen to who a person really is. That is who you are really going to spend your life with, not the illusion that you create in your own mind.

Speaking

Speaking is the next part of communication. Taking care of someone means choosing your words very carefully. Just "letting it all hang out" can be very damaging in a relationship. Saying mean things to each other, especially when you are angry, can cause irreparable harm. There is never a good excuse, and saying you're sorry doesn't take away the pain that you have caused.

Learning to control your anger and your words *before* you hurt someone will not only give you a stronger relationship, but your partner will also learn to think before hurting you as well. People often indulge themselves by letting their anger lash out of control, and then justify it afterward by saying, "They deserved it." Be aware of your own inclination to do this. Part of caring for someone is protecting that person from being hurt, including protecting that person from being hurt by you. Uncontrollable anger governs cases we have all heard about: alcohol abusers who get drunk and either physically or verbally abuse their families. The abuse is often followed by a showering of gifts and affection, and begging for forgiveness. This pattern is as dysfunctional for the abuser as it is for the family.

One story I heard was about a woman whose husband kept verbally abusing her. She not only felt sorry for him, but she believed his accusations that it was her fault that he was abusive. He said that if she managed the children better, and made more money at her job, he wouldn't be so stressed all the time. It took eight months of therapy (kept secret from her husband), for her to build up the courage to try to stop the abuse. But when her attempts made her husband even worse, she quit the therapy, and just took the abuse. It makes me sad to think about the dysfunctional patterns that their children will grow up with. I wish this woman had been strong enough to stand up for herself and show her husband the long-term ramifications of his actions.

Every word we utter has a cause and an effect. Every time we open our mouths, our words have an effect on someone or something. It would be very valuable if we could see how our words affect not only other people, but also our own happiness. Maybe you said something a month ago, and your loved one no longer fluffs your pillow at night. Or maybe you don't get flowers as often as you used to. Or maybe your partner is so hurt by the verbal abuse that he or she can no longer trust you. This state of affairs is the result of careless communication. Learning to speak to someone with care and consideration takes time and effort, but the alternative is very sad.

In learning to deliver thoughtful communication, it is also important to say what you really mean. Expressing yourself can be difficult, and even when you are caring, you are often worried about what another will think of you. You might say what you think the other person wants to hear. But in order to develop closeness, you must take a chance that someone cares about what you have to say. If a loved one doesn't, or suppresses you when you try to say what you are thinking or feeling, this *must* be rectified. You must speak about it and resolve the issue, seek joint counseling, or break off a relationship that is damaging to your self-esteem.

Maria, a woman that I used to work with, was the kind of person everyone loved to have around. She always had something nice to say. But as I became more friendly with her over time, I recognized that she was handicapped by her inability to communicate anything that was bothering her. Sometimes her boss would demand that she stay an hour late to work on a big project. But often he had not finished the preparatory work, so she would end up sitting for that extra hour with nothing to do. Or he would invite her to lunch and then cancel at the last minute (usually after the cafeteria was closed), which forced her to eat lunch from a vending machine. But Maria, wanting to be liked and afraid to rock the boat, did not speak up.

What she didn't realize was that she was not doing her boss any favors by letting him abuse her in this way. If she spoke up, not only would she enjoy her work more and probably be more productive because she would let all of her resentments go, but she would also be teaching her boss how to take good care of his employees. He would respect her more for sticking up for herself.

Good communication is vital to a relationship. When things are good, let the other person know. When they're not, talk it out. Even if something seems small and insignificant, get it out in the open. As much damage can be done from withheld communication as from "mean" communication. Withheld information tends to fester and make a person lash out. If you want to say something, and are trying to decide whether you are "being open," versus making a "nasty remark," think about the effects of your words. What is your goal in making the comment? Will it hurt someone, or make your relationship stronger? Remember that your biggest defense against the uncertainty of the future is your ability to communicate with your mate and work things out together.

Actions

Actions are also a very powerful way that people communicate. It can be nothing more than a smile or a pat on the back. Your silence may be telling someone that you are upset, and your body language may be expressing your need for affection. If you are an hour late for dinner without calling, you may be communicating that you don't take your responsibilities seriously. If you leave the dishes in the sink, you may be subtly communicating that you resent having to do so many of the household chores. If you clean someone's closet, you may be letting that person know that you want him or her to feel taken care of. Or, if you rescue your mate from car troubles, you are communicating that he or she can count on you. Pay close attention to the effects of how you communicate your feelings in ways other than speaking. Actions can often be a more valuable way than words to show someone how much you care.

Communication is the main way we take care of other people, and it is a learned skill. Some people do it more naturally than others, but it is based on seeing what other people's needs are, not based on providing what you think they need. It takes time, thoughtfulness, and being willing to really listen to what others want. The most wonderful part about taking care of someone is that it will not only make you feel good, but you will also get someone who takes care of you in return.

Integrity

Integrity may be defined as being who you say you are, and doing what you say you will do. Having integrity is not a natural trait. Society teaches us to do our best to impress people, and that "talk is cheap." So say whatever you want, and do whatever you can get away with. It is therefore quite difficult for someone to learn to have integrity. There are some people whose parents teach them the value of integrity, and some religions focus on this topic, but many people do not know what it is, let alone how to acquire it. Creating integrity in your life is valuable for your own satisfaction, so you can be the kind of person that you can be proud of. It is also critical if you want a relationship that is built on solid ground.

Be Who You Say You Are

Can you imagine the freedom that people would have if they could just be themselves? I don't mean letting all of their emotions run free, I mean being free from trying to impress others, free from trying to prove themselves to people, free from wondering what everyone thinks of them all the time. So many people fear that once people really get to know them, they won't like them. They hide behind their persona in order to avoid this rejection. Some people even fear that they are impostors in their own lives, and one day they will be "discovered." They think that it is just a matter of time before everyone finds out that they are not who they pretend to be. These "shows" that they put on are a result of poor self-esteem. It is not necessarily that they are putting on shows to impress others as much as to hide who they really are from themselves.

Doug is very successful in his career. But even though I met him four years ago, I still feel I don't know him. He is always "on." When you try to have a serious conversation with him, he comes up with amusing quips, or does an imitation of a British aristocrat. I always feel ill at ease when I am with him, and I think it's because he feels ill at ease with himself. Feeling you are an impostor in your own life doesn't need to be this dramatic. But it is very valuable to recognize this quality in yourself. The way out of this situation would probably be to talk to a trained therapist. You need to learn how to be with yourself before you can learn how to be with others.

With regard to the basic "persona" issue that we all have, we need to face up to our lack of authenticity. People often build their relationships on false pretenses. They read into what people want, and instead of being themselves, they become who they think other people want them to be. Or people misrepresent themselves, and then are never free to let their hair down. This game-playing costs them being close to the people to whom they truly want to be closest.

Examples might be a woman who wakes up early in the morning to put on her makeup before her mate wakes up, for fear that he'll see her looking "ordinary." Or a man who is sweet and caring until the day after he's married, and then becomes tyrannical. Or a woman who says to her fiancé before she gets married, "Oh I don't care what religion we raise the kids in. Whatever you want is fine with me." And then this becomes a major issue after the wedding. Or a sweet, submissive person who becomes an angry, aggressive individual after he or she is married. These examples happen every day. That is why it is so important for you to work on your integrity to be who you really are, and not your "persona," so that you can meet someone else who also has this integrity. Real people attract other real people, and this is your *best* chance for lasting happiness.

Once you are self-aware enough to admit that you are not the person that you pretend to be, you will open up the possibility of truly being yourself with others. How exciting! But the big question people ask is, Who am I anyway? To answer this question, turn to question 8 in your notebook. Your mission is to write down a description of yourself with reasonable accuracy, as if you were reporting it to someone else. This is not a description of your looks, your history, your job, your lifestyle, or your value system. It is not a description of who you wish you were (that is who you present in your "persona"). This is a list that accurately describes who you *really* are with no pretenses, judgments, or value systems. Concentrate on your personality traits. What kind of person are you? Introverted? Shy? Responsible? Disorganized? Humorous? A leader? A follower? Carefree? Serious? Stubborn? Kind? Giving? Short-tempered? Thoughtful? Write down all of your strengths and weaknesses.

Being objective about how you describe yourself, especially with the aspects of yourself that you don't like, is not so easy. Take your time with this description, and keep reviewing it to make sure that you write down what is *true*, not what you wish were true. You can even talk to a close friend and ask him or her how accurate your description is. But remember, that friends are as attached to your "persona" as you are. You may even pick friends who tend to reinforce the image of the person you are pretending to be. So, if you think that your friends will not talk straight to you about this, just do the description yourself. (If you haven't already done so, you should probably do question 8 now before you read on.)

If you're like most people, who you really are and who you pretend to be are quite different. The reason for this is that people are often afraid that their real selves are not good enough. For either rational or irrational reasons, they are afraid to reveal who they really are.

I once read a story about a movie star. She was world famous, and had the world at her feet. Yet she said that no matter how much she accomplished, she always had this nagging feeling of not being "good enough." She saw her drive to succeed as a way to overcome her low self-esteem. The only time she felt that she could truly escape from the feeling was when she became another character on a movie set. But, back in her dressing room, she would still feel she needed to prove her worth to everyone to get their approval.

I thought it was very generous of this actress to share her insecurities so publicly. Many people probably saw themselves in her description. By recognizing your "persona," and seeing the difference between your "persona" and who you really are, you can work on the next step which is to *be* who you really are.

Begin by asking yourself the question, Am I happy with my description of myself? If the answer is yes, then you should have an easier time than most at being yourself with other people. Also, you will not feel the pressure of having to change for someone else. If someone is trying to change you, examine what it is this person is trying to change. If you like the change, and agree that it will not only make you a better person but enhance the relationship as well, then go ahead and begin making the change. If you think this person is trying to change you in ways that you don't like, or that are not constructive, make sure that you discuss your feeling with this person. If the issue is important enough, and this person won't stop trying to change you, consider ending the relationship. You don't need anyone in your life who is destructive to your growth process.

If the answer is no, that you are not happy with your description of yourself, or parts of it, then you have a bit more work to do. There are basically three options that you can take. The first is to do nothing and continue to be unhappy. Many people do this, yet continue to pretend to be someone else. They know who they are, but they don't want to make the effort to change. Not only will they continue to be miserable, but their relationships will be also.

The second option is to work on yourself to change the part of the description that you don't like. This is actually a bit easier than it sounds. If you are shy, besides reading self-help books, finding outgoing role models, and going to therapy, the most efficient way to change something about yourself is to *practice* being the way you want to be! It is amazing how powerful this is. Try it once, and you will see how well it works!

It is also important not to confuse "putting on a show" with practicing a trait in order to change and grow. The difference is that with the former you are not being straight with people, in the latter, you are straightforward. For example, if you meet someone while you are practicing being responsible, you should tell them, "Listen, I am working very hard to be more responsible. I haven't always been this way, but with effort, I hope to change for the better." That person will respect you more than you thought possible.

The third option is not to change the personality trait within yourself that you don't like, but to change your *opinion* about that personality trait. Often times, people dislike characteristics about themselves for no good reason. Maybe their siblings always made fun of them for being so nice, and so in their personas they act unkind and tough. Think back to how you came to dislike a particular aspect of yourself, and even have a friend or therapist assist you in analyzing it objectively. Is it truly an undesirable trait, or have you just been programmed to think it is? If you think that being a follower is bad, question why. Being a follower can be a very good quality in terms of getting a job done. Why do you think it is bad? Being objective about your qualities will allow you the freedom to be the way you are already, to stop thinking it is wrong to be this way, and to stop pretending to be something different. When you have integrity, and are true to yourself, you have the power and freedom to be who you are.

Do What You Say You Will Do

The other critical factor in having integrity is to do what you say you will do. Don't you hate it when others don't do what they say they will? What is it about people not keeping their promises that makes us not trust them? Why do we berate politicians for not keeping their campaign promises? If you look to the people in the world who have made the most significant contributions, many of their greatest triumphs came from doing what they said they were going to do. Why do we so value a woman volunteer who shows up at the hospital at six o'clock every morning without fail? The reason is that dependability is one of the most valuable traits a human being can have.

It is also very rare. Once you see how many promises you and others make that aren't followed through on, or even intended to be followed through on, you will be shocked. The first step toward learning to keep your word is being aware of when you don't keep it. So many people schedule meetings at two, three, and four o'clock—each appointment at opposite ends of town. They forget to schedule traveling time and spread themselves too thin. They are late all day, and miserable. This is one area in which thinking and planning ahead makes an enormous difference. To do what you say you will do takes a great deal of determination and practice. Not only do you need to be very careful about what you promise to do, but once you do make a promise, you need to remember it in order to follow through on it.

A good way to start practicing keeping your word might be to get a little notebook and write down all of the promises you make. For instance, if you say to someone, "Let's do lunch," follow up on it. If you tell someone you will arrive at noon, write it down. When you tell someone you are going to send him or her a book, write it in your notebook, and then do it. And when you break your promise, it is very important to admit that you have broken it, apologize for it, and do whatever you need to do to make it up to that person.

Trust
Trust takes time to develop, yet it is a vital part of being close to someone. When you have trust in a relationship, you not only have the freedom to be yourself and to communicate without fear of retribution, but also something very powerful happens: you lose the fear of the future. When you don't trust someone, you are constantly afraid that person will harm you in some way. Examples of this might be fear that your partner will say something mean to you, that he or she won't be there when you really need someone, or that he or she will embarrass you in front of others. All of your actions are then in "defensive" mode, because you're just waiting for your partner to hurt you.

Many people learned to distrust others because of how they were treated by their parents. The parents would say one thing and do another. Or parents would be sweet one minute and angry the next. And often people feel that they have no one that they can really count on, not even themselves.

A young girl named Adrienne was at a dinner party her parents were hosting, and I was seated next to her. She was very nicely dressed. She said all of the correct things, and ate with fine table manners. She did not utter a word out of turn, nor did she even ask for more juice when her glass was empty. There was nothing about this girl that was childlike in any way. She was not playful or curious, and didn't even speak with the other girls at the table. Then something occurred that I happened to notice. Someone had told a joke, and Adrienne laughed out heartily, inadvertently revealing the contents of food in her mouth. Her mother gave her the most awesome glare that even sent a shiver down my spine!

I am the first to agree with solid discipline for children, but this girl is living in a frightening environment. Her parents lack the trust in their daughter that she will behave well (or at least suitably for her age). And in turn, they have created a young girl who cannot trust them to be forgiving of her mistakes. The lack of trust in this relationship not only makes for a very tense living environment, but it also creates a situation which makes it very difficult for them to be close to each other.

Becoming Trust Neutral

It is very valuable to learn about your own ability to trust. You probably fall into one of three categories. The first category is that you are too trusting of people. You tend to believe everything a person says, and then end up getting hurt. The second category is that you are the mistrusting kind. No matter how trustworthy a person is, you cannot trust him or her, and you feel that most people are not trustworthy. The third category is that you are neutral upon first meeting someone. You make every effort to get to know this person and then determine whether or not he or she is trustworthy. Look at yourself closely to determine in which category you fit. If you are not reasonably close to neutral, then you have a problem that you need to work on.

A good way to try to become more neutral is to try to figure out how you got to be the way you are with regard to trust. Look back to your past, and try to see why you might be the way you are. It might be easier if you speak to a friend or therapist, or read a self-help book on the subject. Discovering why you are the way you are is very important in creating yourself to be the way you would prefer to be. Once you see the root of the problem, you can work toward being neutral, which will take time and patience. Pick out role models to emulate, practice being neutral, and even push yourself to the opposite extreme for practice. The more neutral you are upon meeting someone, the better you will be at developing a solid, trusting relationship. Rather than prejudging someone's trustworthiness, you can discover if that person is someone who truly deserves to be trusted.

Gary's mother died when he was seven years old. He found it very hard to trust women, maybe because subconsciously he felt they would all leave him one day. He was very confrontational with his girlfriend all the time, almost as if he wanted to push her away before she could leave him. When his girlfriend, who was very insightful, told him that she thought that he just didn't trust women because his mom had "left" him, he denied this as a possibility. But after many such discussions, he started to acknowledge that there was some truth to it. Just seeing this clearly for the first time opened up a new world for him.

It helped him on the journey from being untrustworthy to being more neutral. This transition helped him to become closer to his girlfriend than he had been to anyone. He even found that he was able to delegate more work to his secretary, and trust her to complete it accurately. Growing toward being neutral deepens all the relationships that one has.

Once you are neutral, your job in your relationship is to observe and discover whether or not your mate is reliable. Does your mate keep promises? Act consistently? Demonstrate caring for you? Can you count on your mate? Will this person be there when you need someone? Does this person tell the truth?

Also important in a relationship is how a person reacts when he or she is angry. Can you trust your mate to still "take care of the relationship" even when he or she gets angry? Can you count on your mate to work out anger in a constructive way, or might he or she take it out on you, either physically, by getting drunk, or by having an affair? Does your partner indulge in "temporary insanity" and then apologize afterward even though the damage has already been done?

Really look at these characteristics in a person. Not only do you need to give your mate every possible chance of being trusted by you (by starting out neutral), but your mate also has to act trustworthy in order to earn your trust. In addition, you need to examine for yourself how trustworthy you are. Can people count on you? Do you keep your word? These are certainly areas to work on, and the more trustworthy you are, the more trustworthy a mate you will find.

It is important to keep in mind that both you and your mate will have occasional lapses. Not everyone is perfect. What is important for you to look for in a mate (and important for you to provide) is a willingness to admit and recognize that he or she made a mistake, and a willingness to do whatever is necessary to rectify the situation. For instance, if you were counting on your mate to take you out to dinner as promised, beware if your mate says instead, "Oh, it was only a suggestion. I feel like staying home tonight." This person is not trustworthy. Now if this person says, "Listen, I *know I promised* to take you out tonight, but I am really exhausted. I apologize. Can I please take you somewhere really special tomorrow night?" he or she would be considered trustworthy. The latter person broke the promise just as did the former, but was honest about it, and made up for it.

Trust Takes Time

In order for a genuine trust to develop, a person must have many, many opportunities to prove his or her trustworthiness. That is why it is so important that you take your time at the beginning of a relationship. The other person needs time to earn your trust. Too many people try to skip this vital process and settle for a Hollywood-style pseudo-intimacy rather than establishing mutual trust, respect, and genuine caring. They give up deep, meaningful relationships; they would rather be enchanted for an evening by someone they don't really know. To be sure, this can be very exciting at the time, but we're better off not talking about how they feel the next morning.

People get so swept away by romance that they don't think clearly. Romance is a fantasy. It is wonderful and one of life's great pleasures, but unless there is a great deal of trust between the two engaging in the fantasy, one person often gets hurt. When the veil of fantasy is lifted, and we discover that the person we were imagining doesn't really exist, the pain can be tremendous. Save the romance for the trusting, stable relationship of the future. Right now, focus on getting to know who the person *really* is.

One of the reasons this issue is so difficult is that we confuse sexual tension with deeper emotions. We misinterpret mutual physical desire as a sign that the other person is "right" for us, and vice versa. Too often, we don't even know who this person is! We are just reacting to who we think and wish the person might be. Only weeks later do we realize our mistake. Remember, you can never take back what has already been done.

If that sexual tension is not there on a first date, avoid the temptation to dismiss the person. In a stable, healthy relationship you will feel completely comfortable with someone and be able to really be yourself. Many long-married couples report exceptionally high levels of sexual satisfaction, but this isn't based on sexual tension. It is simply based on knowing someone very well. Remember this when you go on a date with someone who matches all the items on your list, but seems to supply no sexual "charge."

Going slowly and taking your time to get to know and trust someone is the key to developing a solid, stable relationship. It may be the opposite of how you have always done things, and it may take willpower and determination, but your future depends on it. If this person is truly "the one," don't you want all of your memories with him or her to be extra special? And if you are serious about getting married, would you really want to marry the kind of person who would jump into bed with someone on the first date? Ask yourself: Do you think a decent and honorable person would want to marry you if you offered to jump into bed on the first night? That person might jump in, too, but odds are that he or she won't marry you.

Obviously, there are exceptions to this rule, but it's not worth taking the chance of blowing what could be a fabulous relationship that could lead to marriage by "trusting" someone you don't know, rushing physical intimacy, and then waiting to see how it will turn out and hoping for the best. Take control of your own life and your own emotional stability by taking control of your own body. Don't risk waking up the next morning thinking you blew it. Most of the time you will be right.

When *is* the appropriate time to become sexually intimate with someone? In an ideal world, the best time would be to wait until after marriage. Being sexually intimate with a person distorts your ability to decide whether a person is right for you; your emotions get in the way of making an objective choice and cause a great deal of confusion. Selecting a partner based on sexual attraction will lead you down the same path that you may already know well—great times (for a while), no commitment. There is only one way to avoid this: select your mate using your master list, and *keep sex out of the picture.* This ensures that you are choosing each other as lifetime partners for the most important reasons: you match each other's master lists, you share similar values, and you have similar visions for the future.

Lori recognized in herself the need to feel loved by the people she dated. She equated sexual intimacy with love, and always ended up being disappointed that it didn't satisfy her need for love. When she looked back on her past relationships, Lori realized that she had put her physical desires and her desire to be loved before her emotional needs of security and stability. She felt a great deal of remorse. She wished she could take back every time she had been sexually intimate with a man, knowing that she had slept with men for all the wrong reasons. She felt that the only way she could make sure that a man truly loved her and was right for her was to be sure that the two of them got to know each other without the emotional rollercoaster sex always puts her on. She made the decision to wait until she met and married "the one" before becoming intimate again. This is not an easy decision, especially considering that she had been intimate so easily before. I spoke with Lori a few months after she made her decision, and she admitted that it was extremely difficult. Not only did she have to get over her own desperate attempts to get love from men through intimacy, but she had to be very strong against the pressure that men put on her. She told me that seeing things from her new perspective made it excruciatingly clear how much emphasis is put on sexual "chemistry" in our society. She is now trying to work hard on *not* using this as her guide to find a mate.

Another reason to wait until after marriage is that by becoming intimate before marriage you forfeit a substantial incentive for someone to marry you and reduce the sense of urgency. (This is especially true if you are seeing someone who has a history of avoiding commitment.) Why marry someone if you get everything you want without having to commit? When you are married, there is a high level of trust and security, you know each other very well, you have a solid commitment to each other, and you know that the relationship won't disappear overnight. This is very comforting to people who have been in relationships where they were in constant fear about what their partner would do. By waiting, you protect yourself, you strengthen the relationship, and you create a closeness that cannot be attained in any other way.

But many people feel the need to sleep with someone to see if they are sexually compatible. The problem is that if someone matches every other item on your master list, and you are not sexually compatible, your instinct may be to drop this person quickly. This is tragic, not only because people often put too much emphasis on one sexual experience, but also because the most significant aspect of sexual compatibility is communication. Communication takes trusting one another, love for one another, and most importantly, time. Perhaps this person could make a fabulous mate for you; with a bit of communication, he or she may have the potential to be the most sexually compatible partner imaginable. Too often, we look for instant gratification and have the mistaken idea that if this is "the one," then everything should be perfect. How many times have you been incredibly sexually compatible with someone only to find that the relationship was terrible or didn't last? Using the excuse of sleeping with someone before marriage in order to "determine compatibility" is not a reliable approach; you can almost always work things out through communication later on.

Unfortunately, we live in a society in which the norm is to engage in intimacy early on in a relationship. If you are unable or unwilling to wait until marriage, you should at an absolute minimum wait for at least three or four months before becoming intimate with someone. That is the minimum amount of time it will take for you to discover whether someone is consistently trustworthy or not. A person can say anything to you for his or her own purposes, including "I love you" and "I want to marry you." After you have sex, what are you going to do when you learn your partner now feels differently about the relationship? Restraint for these four months will help you gain a significant amount of intimacy in other areas of the relationship, determine this person's dedication to the relationship, and decide whether you as a couple are ready to be exclusive with each other. Waiting lets the other person know that you value yourself and the relationship. If your date pressures you, you know right away what this person *really* wants from the relationship. If, on the other hand, this person is kind and caring without sleeping with you, then you know that his or her actions are genuine, and you have probably found a good candidate for marriage. Isn't that the kind of person with whom you would want to raise children?

If you go on a date with someone you are sure is not "the one," you may see no harm in spending the night with them. Obviously, this is up to you. But I don't think people are willing to admit how much emotional attachment goes into so called "casual" sex. I don't think "casual sex" exists. People want to believe it does in order to justify their unwillingness to take responsibility for their own actions, but it is hard to deny the emotional turmoil that these "casual" relationships entail. Ask yourself: Can you afford to have more "dangling" relationships following you around? You have a mate to find. Why let anything stand in your way!

As a member of a society that is addicted to instant fulfillment, you will stand out from the crowd if you make it clear that you are someone who honors delayed gratification. This approach will attract the kind of mate who is looking for a deep, caring, trusting relationship based on mutual respect. But this course will also be difficult for you, because people who do not share your views will tell you that there is something wrong with you. Let them repeat their diagnosis to you when you are in a trusting, respecting, strong marriage—and they are still floating around looking for the newest instantaneously gratifying date.

Commitment

Commitment is the fourth cornerstone of a stable relationship. Being committed means that you will make the relationship work through good times and bad. It is very valuable to examine what stops you from staying committed. Take a look back at your past relationships and examine how they ended. What role did you play in their demise? Sometimes, people have a pattern of "bailing out" when they get too close in relationships. They are scared of the intimacy relationships bring, and are afraid that others will let them down. Or maybe they think they are committed, but they aren't willing to work so hard to make relationships work. They are under the mistaken notion that if it's right it should be "easy." Whatever the case, getting committed to a relationship is a conscious decision that you make, and staying committed takes work. The good news is that once you are committed, not only does the relationship become stronger, but your efforts in the relationship become habits that become easier to perform.

Making a commitment to a person and to a relationship takes an enormous amount of courage and is a scary process. This is often where people who want to get married back off. It's like standing at the top of a tall diving board ready to jump, and turning around and going back down the ladder. This is a very normal and natural feeling. Or sometimes people jump right in, head first, without thinking. This is also a mistake because it isn't until much later that they realize that their thoughtlessness cost them years in bad relationships.

That is why it is so important to take the time to get to know someone before you do make this commitment. Getting to know someone takes much more time and effort than anyone is willing to admit. In our society of immediate gratification, we judge people by what they seem to be on the surface. That is one of the reasons that so many marriages end unhappily. If people would only take the time *before* they get married to really get to know their prospective partners, the world would be a much healthier and happier place.

The time that you spend together is very precious, and how you lay the bricks of this new relationship will determine the home that you live in later. That is why it is so important to go slowly, and to take very good care of how you progress in the relationship. Take every step with deliberation and forethought. By going slowly, the fear and the tendency to act without thinking will be lessened, and you can develop a relationship that is built on solid ground. Also, by moving slowly, a certain amount of time will pass. Since life has its ups and downs, you are bound to go through difficult times together. It is incredibly valuable to see how you support each other in times like these. Not only will it show you if you work well together, but what the quality of your marriage will be in the future.

In the process of making a commitment, it is important that your partner is working toward making the same type of commitment. The decision to have an "exclusive" relationship cannot be rushed, and it is obviously much better if both of you make this decision at the same time. Whether that means that one of you speeds up your own readiness, or the other one slows down, this is an important area of compromise. Another way to make the commitment process a bit easier is to see each other only at scheduled times so that you both don't feel overwhelmed.

When Roger first met Marcy, he had a feeling that she might be "the one." It really made him nervous. After seeing her almost every night for five weeks, he began to feel walls closing in on him. He almost called the whole relationship off. He made a very smart move, however, by calling his uncle to get support. His uncle suggested that he slow the whole process down so that he could handle it a lot easier.

Roger then took Marcy out to dinner, and told her that he was very serious about pursuing the relationship, but that it was going a bit too fast for him. And, in order to move forward comfortably, he would like to see her only twice per week. Marcy was quite upset at first because she felt that everything was going along beautifully. She did understand how he felt, and wanted to accommodate him, but she had her own insecurities to deal with as well. She told him that if she agreed to this, she needed for Roger to really show his seriousness by seeing her exclusively. They finally compromised and agreed to exclusivity in two months time if all went well. This proved to be a very good solution, and the couple are now happily married!

Making a commitment may take a lot of patience. There are obstacles to overcome, and you may be skeptical of a relationship because you fear that maybe the person isn't really "it." Sometimes making a commitment means making the person "it." Sometimes you just need to get over your own inability to act, and just make the commitment. And sometimes, you just need to hang in there and be patient with your mate. Your care and consideration for this person while he or she is getting over the inability to act will mean more to this person than you can know. Maybe one too many people has given up.

Being committed to someone during turbulent times makes a relationship strong. Part of being someone's partner is to be strong when the person feels weak, or let the person support you when you are not at your best. And being a partner means staying committed to someone even when you are in the middle of working out major problems together. Sometimes a solution comes through teamwork; sometimes it comes through compromise. Constructive problem-solving means working it out together with a firm commitment from each of you to stick it out. Turbulent times call for extraordinary compassion on each of your parts, and if you learn from these times, learn from your mistakes, and learn from hanging in there with someone, your relationship will be stronger than you ever thought possible.

NOTEBOOK

1. In what ways could you improve your listening skills?

_____

_____

_____

_____

_____

_____

_____

2. How do you plan to accomplish this?

_____

_____

_____

_____

_____

_____

_____

3. In what ways could you improve your speaking skills?

_____

_____

_____

_____

_____

_____

4. How do you plan to accomplish this?

_____

_____

_____

_____

_____

_____

5. In what ways could you use your actions to communicate that you care about your partner?

_____

_____

_____

_____

_____

_____

6. Are you willing to recognize that you do have a "persona"?

_____

7. Are you committed to "being yourself"?

_____

8. Describe yourself as if you are reporting it to someone else. Concentrate on your personality traits—introverted, organized, a follower.

_____

_____

_____

_____

_____

9. Are you happy with this description?

_____

10. If not, what do you plan to change about yourself?

_____

_____

_____

_____

_____

_____

11. Or, if not, what opinions do you plan to change about yourself?

_____

_____

_____

_____

_____

_____

12. How often do you notice that you don't keep your word?

_____

13. What do you plan to do to improve this situation?

_____

_____

_____

_____

_____

14. How trusting are you (not at all, too much, neutral)?

_____

15. How do you plan to become more neutral?

_____

_____

_____

_____

_____

_____

_____

16. How do you plan to be a better judge of trustworthiness?

_____

_____

_____

_____

_____

_____

_____

_____

17. How trustworthy are you? Can people count on you?

_____

_____

18. Do you tend to rush your relationships without giving trust a chance to develop?

_____

19. How do you intend to overcome this?

_____

_____

_____

_____

_____

_____

_____

20. What stops you from being committed in relationships?

_____

_____

_____

_____

_____

_____

_____

21. How do you plan to grow in terms of your ability to make a commitment?

_____

_____

_____

_____

_____

_____

_____

22. What insights have you learned in this chapter that will make you better at developing stable relationships?

_____

_____

_____

_____

_____

_____

9

Getting Engaged

THESE WORDS ARE both thrilling and frightening at the same time! They bring up the vision of a man getting down on one knee, handing a woman a velvet box, and as he gazes into her eyes, asking, "Will you marry me?" This exact scenario may not happen to you. But what is most important is that this relationship that you have been working so hard to find and develop culminates in a marriage proposal. That is your purpose and your goal.

Meet Friends and Family
There are a few things you should do *before* you get engaged. The first is to meet each other's friends and family. You've heard it a thousand times: When you marry someone, you marry that person's whole family. This may not be important to you now, but when your mate takes your father-in-law's side of an argument against you, or your sister-in-law starts telling you how to run your affairs, you will quickly realize the involvement of the rest of the family in a marriage. It is good to know this before you say "I do."

In the best of circumstances, your combined families can provide a support system and stability in your relationship that you can't get anywhere else. Or a family can interfere and make life very difficult for your relationship. The majority of families fall somewhere in between, but it is wise for you to get to know a potential partner's family so that you will be prepared for your future. No matter how great your relationship, his or her family has the potential to make your life miserable.

And if your mate meets your family and makes derogatory comments, you need to think twice about whether you want to put up with that for the rest of your life. Or if members of your family pull you aside and tell you that you are making the biggest mistake of your life, you need to at least listen. Unless you have real reason to question family members' motives for saying this, you need to take their input very seriously.

Peggy said that she was very upset because she introduced her boyfriend, Ted, to her family, and everyone wanted her to break up with him. She was very serious with him, and they had discussed marriage several times. This situation is not uncommon, and it is very difficult to rectify. Peggy really felt that she was in a position where she would have to choose Ted over her family. And how could she give him up? She was so blissfully happy with him when they were together.

She could see her family's objections: Ted was eighteen years her senior, had three grown kids whom he didn't pay much attention to, he was adamant that he didn't want any more children, and he was often out of work because he had a hard time working with people. But Peggy felt that no one could really understand how wonderful he made her feel, and how much fun they had together. Yes, she wanted children, but she sincerely felt that she could change his mind.

I wish I had been close enough to Peggy to tell her that you just don't marry someone solely because you are "blissful" together. That is a temporary "feeling," and a very weak foundation for a relationship. One day, she would wake up and realize that she was with someone who had a totally different vision for life than she did. He didn't have the stability she would need for raising children, and only if she were very lucky would her family come back to catch her when she fell.

A few months later, a mutual friend shared with me what had happened to Peggy and Ted's relationship. One night, Ted came over for dinner, and he had apparently had too much to drink. The evening started off well because Peggy thought his behavior was hysterically funny. She enjoyed pampering him, and he was talking non-stop about their friends, making the funniest comments. It was not until after dinner, when his high was winding down, that he began to denigrate her family. He said some absolutely horrible things about her sister and her mother. At first Peggy began to defend them, but then she just began to cry. And the more she cried, the more horrible he got.

At about nine o'clock that night, Peggy's roommate came home, and she asked Ted to leave, which he did. The next day, Peggy and her sister took all of his things from her apartment, packed them in a box, and left them in his apartment with his key, and a note ending the relationship. Our mutual friend said that Peggy considers herself extremely fortunate to have had the opportunity to extricate herself from the relationship when she did. And even though a family can sometimes be meddlesome, it always pays to listen to your loved ones, because they might just be right, and they almost always have your best interest at heart.

Getting to know your partner's friends is a good idea, too. If your mate is one way with you, and acts completely different around friends, what is this person really like? What is this person hiding that you may only find out about after the wedding? What are your mate's friends' character traits? If they aren't people with whom you would enjoy spending time, you must discuss this with your mate so that the two of you can come to a compromise. This is not the most vital issue of whether you should marry this person or not, but it is important to have an understanding about each other's friends from the beginning.

Don't Live Together
Living together is neither really living, nor really being together. Your objective is to get married. The moment you live with your mate, all of the incentive to get married goes out the window! If your mate wants to be able to spend more time with you, the only way your mate can do that is by marrying you! If you live with him or her you are taking one huge gamble. Your mate's sense of urgency completely disappears, and when you bring the subject up, your mate will roll his or her eyes and say, "Not that again." Don't degrade yourself by putting yourself in that position. If your mate really wants to be with you, there is one and only one way to achieve that—through marriage.

Or, maybe it is you who is pursuing the idea to live together. Try to examine the reasons why. Are you afraid to be alone? Are you afraid your mate is going out with someone else? Do you find it more convenient? These insecurities and the need for immediate gratification are very poor beginnings for a stable relationship.

I know that there are many people who disagree with me on this. I have a friend named Michael who thinks that I am very old-fashioned. He moved in with his girlfriend, and now they are engaged. I am very happy for them, and there are many cases where this kind of situation works out. Not only do I feel that living together really inhibits a couple's determination to make a commitment, but that if two people live together, and it doesn't work out, it takes much longer for them to extricate themselves from the situation and begin to date again.

The couple may also break up for the wrong reasons. She may feel he doesn't keep the place neat enough, or he may feel that she stays at work too late. In a marriage, there is a level of commitment that makes compromising easier. Compatibility in marriage is entirely different from the "checking each other out" mentality of living together. When you make the full-blown commitment to get married, when even a little problem arises, you are forced to work it out rather than to "bail."

Living together is having it all with no commitment. That is the worst possible scenario for a relationship to succeed! You are simply setting yourself up for failure. Perhaps it's not such a coincidence that at the same time as living together got popular in America, there was a huge increase in the divorce rate, another sign of lack of commitment to relationships.

Discuss the Details

The next step before you get engaged is to make sure that you have a discussion on the basics of how you want to live your lives together. So many people assume that if a relationship works, all the petty aggravations of life will somehow just solve themselves. And then they are disappointed when they don't. In fact, often times, it is the little details that cause the greatest problems after the fact. Before you get engaged to someone, it is very valuable to talk about how you would like to live your lives together.

Talk about how many kids you want, what religion you want to practice, how you want to raise kids, where you want to live, who will take care of what housework, what each of your responsibilities will be in terms of working outside the house, who will pay the bills, and how you will organize your finances.

Julie was Jewish, and she was marrying Brandon, who was Christian. The two of them had discussed the issue, but not fully. They had decided that since neither one of them was religious, they would raise their family nonreligiously, and at the age of fifteen, their kids could decide what religions they wanted to practice. They also decided to celebrate both Christmas and Hanukkah, not as religious events, but as American holidays.

But they did not discuss this topic thoroughly enough. With only a few months to the wedding, they were still arguing about who would officiate at the wedding. Both families were in on these discussions, and it was becoming unpleasant. They also had not discussed whether their children would be baptized or whether there would be a bris. They didn't discuss where they would send their kids to school, what they would do if one of the mothers-in-law bought them little Stars of David or crosses to wear around their necks, or how they would deal with questions on the subject that the kids would have when they came home from school. They didn't decide what they would do for all of the other holidays like Passover and Easter, or most importantly, what they would do if in the future either person had the desire to turn to his or her religion for spiritual support. Without full discussions of these issues, they are bound to run into many difficulties which could be lessened considerably by discussing them before marriage.

All of these different issues don't need to be decided in perfect detail, but it is important that the two of you have a general consensus. By discussing it, you are giving yourself the best shot at success. But even after you've covered these basic topics, you're not necessarily home free. Often times, in a courting relationship, the two people progress at different speeds, and this can be difficult to handle. To follow are several different scenarios that can take place, and some ideas on how to handle them.

You're Ready, Your Mate's Not

Finally you've found the best mate in the world for you. This person matches your list, he or she has strong character traits, and you've developed a stable relationship together. So what's wrong? This has got to be one of the most frustrating times for you after all that you have gone through to get this far.

What you must do, however, is to realize that if this person fits your list so well, and your relationship is a strong one, then you have to go on the premise that this person is "the one." The worst thing you can do right now is to back down, start questioning yourself, and wonder if you are mistaken. You have your criteria; you have your standards. You wouldn't have let this relationship get this far if it didn't fit your plan of getting married. At this point you have to make a commitment to yourself to do whatever it takes to make it work with this person. You must focus all of your energy to move this relationship toward marriage.

The first step, and what may seem obvious, is to sit down and talk about it. If you have not already done so, tell your mate that you love him or her. Sometimes that is all it takes for someone to be reassured enough to be willing to make the commitment to marriage. Or tell your mate that you want to spend the rest of your lives together. Maybe your persistence is what your partner needs to overcome his or her fears. Ask your partner what he or she sees for your future together. Discuss commitment, and the possible fear of it. The basic goal is to move the conversation in the direction of making a commitment. You must be very gentle so that you don't make your mate feel too much pressure, but you also want to be straightforward. Your mate may not commit at that exact moment, but hopefully the conversation will get him or her thinking about it.

Julian, who has been married for two years, told me that when he was courting Meredith, who was younger than he, she wasn't even thinking about marriage. It wasn't until Valentine's Day when he wrote her a beautiful love letter that she came to understand how serious he was. He said that their relationship was not the same after that day. She stopped dating other men, and within four months he proposed to her.

Another way to move the relationship forward is to become less available to your partner. This sounds a little bit like game-playing, but game playing is something that you do behind someone's back. In this case you are very straightforward. Tell your partner that you are interested in making a commitment, and that you feel that by pulling away a little, he or she will miss you and realize how important you are. Instead of seeing your mate for both weekend nights, keep it down to just one. Go to the movies with your friends on the other night. Don't date other people at this point, and let your mate know that you don't intend to date others so he or she will feel secure about your intentions. This will probably be excruciatingly difficult for you because, if you love this person, you will want to be together all the time. But this is a powerful way for your mate to realize how much he or she needs you, and hopefully it won't take too long before your mate is ready to commit to marriage.

The amount of time it will take you and your mate to know each other well enough to commit to marriage is approximately three to nine months. If you have gone out for this length of time and have tried everything to get your mate to commit—such as communicating, empathizing, and making him or her feel safe to express feelings—and you are no further along towards a commitment of marriage, then you have three choices: continue waiting for another three to six months, give an ultimatum, or break off the relationship.

Waiting for an additional three to six months may be risky, but if your partner seems very serious about the relationship, but claims just to need more time, it may be worth the risk. Just be sure that he or she has proven trustworthy, so that when you hear, "I just need more time," you can trust that it's true.

The second choice, giving an ultimatum, is not pleasant, but sometimes there is no other way to push a person into action. This needs to be carried out with tact, gentleness, and open communication. Let your partner know that you are not trying to exercise your power, but you are trying to ensure that you are not wasting your time. You are interested in a permanent relationship. It is very important to be absolutely clear about the exact date that your partner must commit by, and about the consequences if he or she does not commit by that date. Consequences may include breaking off the relationship, not seeing them for one month, or maybe seeing them only once per week. You must stick to this consequence *no matter how difficult it is for you.* If you do not adhere to your own pronouncements, you will be in a much weaker position than you were before the ultimatum. Further, you will not be able to use this strategy again, because it won't hold any power over your mate. Perhaps worst of all, you won't believe your ultimatum yourself. Before making an ultimatum, be very sure you intend to carry it out. Ultimatums not only serve to push your mate into action, but also push *you* to move on when you aren't getting a commitment.

The third choice is to break off the relationship. Many people date someone they think is the right one for a long time, and they wait and hope that this person will eventually commit. But if it has been six to twelve months and you are not engaged, then it doesn't matter how *right* the person seems. He or she does not have the one essential quality—the ability to commit to you. The right one *will* commit. Clinging to a person who has everything going for him or her except the ability to commit is agonizing and will keep you from getting married. Break off the relationship now before you waste any more precious time.

Your Mate's Ready, You're Not
Making a commitment takes a great deal of courage and conviction. Even when you know it is what you really want, have it all written

down on paper, and have worked very hard to find someone, when someone wants to marry you, it is very scary! Suddenly, you see your whole future lying in front of you. Sure it is a future you want, but it can be frightening.

Sandra said that while she knew Keith was the perfect man for her, and she loved him very much, marrying him would mean moving to San Francisco. She just didn't feel ready to leave her life in Los Angeles, and she also was concerned about giving up her "independent" status. While she was committed to getting married, she enjoyed the relationship a lot, and didn't see why they should rush into marriage.

But after two years in the relationship, Keith wanted to settle down. He was tired of having a long-distance relationship, and he finally gave Sandra an ultimatum that made her very upset. But, it did force her to confront what was stopping her from making the commitment. She told me that there were two obstacles that, at that time, she was unwilling to face. The first was that marrying Keith would mean she was one step closer to having children, a thought that made her very nervous. And the second one was that the thought of depending on someone else made her feel like she was losing "control." By discussing these issues with Keith, and working them through with him, she was finally able to get over these obstacles and commit to marrying him.

The key is to find out what is at the heart of why you aren't ready. Do you think this person isn't "the one"? To see whether this is true or not, or if you are just having last minute jitters, reread your list of ten items of what you are looking for in a mate. Does your mate match many of them? If not, then maybe you're not ready because this person really isn't the right one for you. But if this person does match, then you need to dig deeper into what's stopping you. Turn in your notebook section to question 10 and write down all the reasons you aren't ready to marry this person. Then turn to question 11 and write down all the reasons you would want to marry this person, if you were ready to! Then examine these reasons and see if not committing to getting married is a rational decision, or one based on emotional fear.

Another technique is to give yourself a distinct period of time by when to be ready. An example is, "By September 30, I will be ready to get engaged." You are welcome to share this with your partner or not, but it will get your mind off the fear, and onto a concrete date. The problem with pinpointing a date is that as you near the date you are likely to get more and more anxious. However, from the beginning your commitment has been to get married. Therefore, emotional turmoil or not, you must follow through on your commitment. At the wedding you can laugh about how difficult this decision was for you to make!

Neither of You Is Ready

When you have been dating someone for a long time (at least six months), and you are no closer to marriage than you were three months earlier, this is not a very good sign. If someone matches the items on your list, and has many of the characteristics you seek in a mate, it is crucial to know whether the relationship is really leading toward marriage. Sometimes it may be deceptive, and look like it is heading toward marriage, and sometimes the idea of marriage may just "slip away." You get so comfortable in your daily life with this nice new relationship that you forget all about your goals. All of a sudden a year has gone by, and you are no closer to marriage than you were a year before.

This is terrible, as you have lost a year of your life in terms of developing a stronger relationship with "the one," and you are back where you started. That is why it is valuable to get the ear of a supportive friend who will remind you after two months in a relationship that you are in it with the intention to be married, and who will ask you periodically if it is moving in that direction.

Nancy always talks about how much she wants to get married and start a family. Yet every time I see her, she is with the same man whom she has been with for three years. When we talk privately, she always fills me in on how it's getting closer to marriage, and how much he has changed. Yet, I've been hearing that story for two years. At one time, she had even given him an ultimatum to propose by January or it was over. But January came and went, and she still stuck with him. I just have to assume that even though she says that she's ready to be married, she certainly must not be committed to it.

Discovering that neither of you is ready for marriage may be heartbreaking for you, but the other person may not care at all. Your mate's goal from the beginning may not have ever been to get married, despite what he or she may have told you. If so, you must extricate yourself from this situation as swiftly as possible in order to spend your time finding the real "Mr. or Ms. Right."

If you are right for each other, but neither of you is ready to make the commitment yet, you need to find out why. Is either of you holding out, waiting for someone better to come along? Are you putting it off out of fear? Close communication on this issue is imperative for you to work out whatever is stopping you from making this commitment. It might even take a visit to a counselor to get on your way.

Both of You Are Ready

The most glorious thing in the world is to have two people "find" each other, and want to spend the rest of their lives together! Getting married is one of the biggest life changes that you will ever go through. Not only are you making a commitment to one person, but it's for the rest of your life!

Now, it is vital that you pick a wedding date as soon as possible. It is best if the wedding date is planned no more than three to eight months away in order to keep the momentum going. The moment you become engaged, all of the fears about getting married start filling your head. The only way to counteract this is to fill your head with something far more exciting: wedding plans! By committing to a firm date, you have a focus that keeps you on track.

Now all you have to do is enjoy to the fullest the experience of getting married. Don't hold back one ounce of enthusiasm and joy! Give yourself the freedom to love this person fully and to feel the inner serenity that comes with sharing your future with the best possible mate in the world for you!

NOTEBOOK

1. What has been stopping you from meeting each other's friends?

_____

_____

_____

_____

_____

_____

_____

2. What has been stopping you from meeting each other's families?

_____

_____

_____

_____

_____

_____

_____

3. What problems may have arisen from these meetings?

_____

_____

_____

_____

_____

_____

_____

4. How do you plan to resolve them?

_____

_____

_____

_____

_____

_____

_____

5. How does your partner feel about your unwillingness to live together?

_____

_____

_____

_____

_____

_____

_____

_____

6. Or, what makes you want to live with this person before you make a commitment to each other?

_____

_____

_____

_____

_____

_____

_____

7. What topics would you want to bring up in your conversation with your mate regarding the details of life?

_____

_____

_____

_____

_____

_____

_____

8. If you're ready, and your mate's not, sit down and talk to him or her. What will you say?

_____

_____

_____

_____

_____

_____

_____

9. If your mate is still going too slowly, try to become less available. What efforts will you make to accomplish this?

_____

_____

_____

_____

_____

_____

_____

10. If your mate's ready, and you're not, write down the reasons you think that you may not be ready to get married.

_____

_____

_____

_____

_____

_____

11. Now, write down all the reasons that you would want to marry this person if you were ready to.

_____

_____

_____

_____

_____

_____

12. Write down a distinct date as to when you plan to be ready to be married to this person.

_____

13. If neither of you is ready, and your mate is not planning to ever marry you, get out of the relationship as soon as possible. When do you plan to end the relationship, and how will you do it?

_____

_____

_____

_____

_____

14. Or, if you are right for each other, you need to find out why neither of you is ready.

_____

_____

_____

_____

_____

_____

15. If both of you are ready, be sure to pick a wedding date as soon as possible! What date did you set?

_____

10

Getting Married

YOU'RE FINALLY HERE! What an exciting time it is. There is so much to do, and it all seems to be going so fast. There is a wedding to plan, there are the logistics of moving to arrange, there are emotional issues to deal with, and both of your families are probably right in the middle of everything you do! Managing it all is probably the first big "life project" that the two of you are doing together. There will be difficult decisions to make, many hurdles to overcome, and many special moments to be shared. Enjoy this time thoroughly! It is rich in emotions and will be remembered by both of you for the rest of your lives.

The Wedding

Coping with the logistics of the wedding, whether it is a large or small affair, can put a strain on even the best relationships. When the two of you got engaged, you thought that took a lot of work! But getting married takes much more effort and coordination than people realize. Unless, of course, you have siblings who were married and you played a significant role in the planning. Even then, you probably didn't get the full picture of how much there is to do!

The most efficient way to take care of all the logistical details is to get a divided notebook and in the first few pages make a massive to do list. Then separate each major area that needs to be taken care of and put each of them into different divisions in your notebook. For instance, a subheading called "Possible Wedding Locations," a section for photographers, and a section for cake decorators. Then, under each heading, in the pages that follow, take notes on the information you gather for that topic. There are many excellent books on weddings, and reading them will help take the guesswork out of the planning process.

Dealing with Families

Another very important area that takes a lot of care is dealing with each of your families. There are the strains of the families meeting for the first time that can be very difficult, and will take an enormous amount of patience from you and your mate. Try not to get too upset about issues that come up. Tensions are high, and often situations get blown way out of proportion. Don't let making the wedding list become the next world war. And stay clear of running interference for people as much as you can. Let them work out their problems themselves; you have way too much to do. With any luck, there will be no major problems that can't be resolved with some good old-fashioned communication. Remember that this whole event is to celebrate the union you are making with your mate. Don't let people forget that.

There may be some problems between you and your mate that can be a little difficult to work through. Often, the woman plays the major role in preparing for the wedding. The man usually does a lot, but most of the direction comes from the woman, and the man often plays the supporting role. Sometimes women resent this as they see it as an unfair division of labor. Maybe the man is not being supportive enough. Or sometimes the man feels left out of very important decisions. Maybe he feels that she is not being careful enough in how she spends money.

Conrad was very upset because Laura, his fiancée, and her mother were making many decisions about the wedding that he wanted to be a part of. When Conrad mentioned it to Laura, she didn't take him seriously. She felt that this was her territory, and she almost resented his interference. He finally sat her down and explained to her that he felt left out, and that when she didn't listen to what his needs were, that it really upset him. Only then did Laura start including him in the decisions. Communication here is so vital to the relationship.

These issues really need to be worked out. If the two of you can't work them out by discussing them yourselves, then turn to an older relative, counselor, or your clergyman to assist you in solving them. Remember that even though at the time these issues seem impossible to overcome, somehow you will overcome them, and the relationship is always stronger for having worked them through successfully. And another idea is to try to have one date per week with your fiancé just to enjoy yourselves and not discuss any wedding plans.

Staying Committed

People assume that once they are engaged, life will be wonderful and all their problems will disappear. But just as it took a great deal of effort to build a stable relationship, it takes a lot to keep it stable. During this stressful time all of the insecurities and problems that each of you has will come to the surface and will be magnified. You worked so hard to find this person and to make the commitment to marriage, so why all of a sudden does it seem like this person really might not be "the one" after all? Why do you have this urge to extricate yourself from this whole situation? Why is it that you suddenly feel that there is no way you can live with the idiosyncrasies that you once thought were so cute?

Pamela said to me that she felt she was making a horrible mistake. Maybe she just wanted to get married so badly that she settled for the wrong guy. Matt also felt that maybe they were making a mistake. They had already booked a wedding location, and had made most of the wedding arrangements. They were both climbing the walls with worry, and then Matt was unexpectedly sent on a two-week business trip. Pamela told me that when he left, she only took him to the airport as a favor—she wasn't even sad that he was leaving. But by the fourth day, she missed him so much that she was even thinking of flying to Chicago to be with him for the weekend! He was calling her twice a day, and when they finally reunited at the airport on his return, all of their doubts about the marriage were completely gone.

These feelings of doubt are completely normal and are a part of the process of getting married. The question is, how do you handle these feelings so that they don't interfere with your wedding plans?

Talk, Talk, Talk

The best way to get over what people refer to as the "marriage jitters," is talk, talk, and more talk. Your mate is probably going through many of the same fears that you are, and by communicating, the two of you can build a stronger relationship by going through the fears together. Let your mate know that you are totally committed to your relationship, but that these are your feelings, and you need to talk about them so they won't seem so ominous. Ask your mate about his or her feelings, and if he or she is a little scared, too. Don't be rattled if your mate tells you he or she's been having second thoughts and wondering if the two of you are really making the right decision. Just say, "Yes we are," and let your mate know that you are sure that these feelings that you are both having are perfectly natural, and that together the two of you can get through them.

If the differences between the two of you are becoming a big problem, you may need to seek a counselor to discuss the issues. This is especially true if you have difficulty talking about the problems, or if you can't have a discussion about them without one or both of you getting angry. Working out these problems is your first real test of how you will cope with difficulties once you are married. Just remember, to be committed is to let nothing stand in your way. As a team, the two of you can and must get on the other side of whatever is holding you back. Make use of Chapter 8 to strengthen your own convictions about working together and staying committed.

There is one caveat to talking to your mate. If you are really scared (even though you know that what you really want is to marry this person, but your old pattern—the "bail syndrome"—is making you want out) do not talk to your mate about this. It will only scare your mate more, and for no good reason. Find someone—a friend, a therapist, an acquaintance who has been through what you're going through—and talk it out with that person. Sometimes these momentary "panic attacks" will even go away overnight, and you will wake up the next morning totally recommitted to the relationship. Don't talk to your mate about it unless it is real and serious, and the feeling doesn't go away in time or by talking to someone. These are very normal feelings, and you are strong enough to overcome them. Just remember what you are committed to, and make use of the support around you to talk about the difficulties you are having. Many people go through them.

And, somehow, working hard on planning the wedding ceremony is the perfect antidote to sitting at home worrying about the decision you just made to marry this person. You become so engrossed in the little details that you don't have time to fret. There is something about the months prior to a wedding that brings out the best and worst in people. People will do things that you won't believe are possible. They will act mean or say horrible things to you. Sometimes a jealous friend will lash out at you, a distant relative will demand to sit at the head table, or a cousin will call to tell you that your fiancé is a terrible match for you. This is part of the weirdness that sometimes surrounds weddings. This is also part of your test to see if you can stay unaffected by it all. Try not to get rattled too much during this time, and don't start any long-term grudges against anyone. If all goes well, you'll be so busy that you won't have time to let things bother you! Just keep your eyes focused on what you're committed to.

Becoming a Team

The process of becoming a team starts with going from the "me" mentality to the "we" mentality. You now have to take your spouse into consideration in every decision you make. You cannot buy a couch on your own, you cannot skip out to the movies without consulting him or her, and you cannot even invite dinner guests over without making sure it's alright. For someone who may have lived for years without this kind of restraint, it may take a bit of adjusting.

There are some people who feel that they are still totally independent, but that now they share some parts of their lives with their spouses. *Wrong.* This will only lead to struggles between you and your partner. You must surrender all of your own agendas and make them less important than those of your joint agenda.

A woman whom I met at a conference told me that she was getting married. She was a successful businesswoman and was very happy to have finally met a great partner. She told me that what she liked so much about him was that he wasn't afraid of her power. She was planning to keep her own name after marriage, was keeping all of her own financial accounts, and had ordered her own personal stationery printed with their new address.

These issues in themselves are fine, but it is the issue underlying them that may be cause for concern. This woman's viewpoint may be caused by her unwillingness to surrender her own identity to that of being "a couple." I admire people who stand up for independence and who don't want to be dependent sloths leaning on someone else for an identity. But in marriage, the key word is interdependence, that is, that you both depend on each other.

This woman needs to start to see herself as part of a team, as the other half of a partnership, not as an "independent being" matched up with another "independent being." This will lead to many conflicts as the two independent beings struggle for dominance and control. A duo of interdependent partners makes for a harmonious, workable marriage.

This may be difficult to do, and it takes time, but in a good solid partnership, the good of the relationship comes before the good of each of you as individuals. This is not to say that you don't have your own "identity." You do. It just falls under the larger umbrella of the relationship.

The Value of Compromise

Another difficult challenge that new couples face is making the compromises necessary to live together peacefully. You may become so attached to your way of doing things that sometimes you don't even realize that you are making something relatively insignificant more important than the one person who is most important to you in the world. Try to keep this perspective in mind when you are arguing about where to store the toothpaste, or how to arrange the furniture. It is important, however, for each of you to give your input on subjects about which you feel strongly. If, in order to avoid an argument, one of you constantly gives in to the other, the resentment will build and affect the relationship negatively.

Lisa said that when she first got married, she thought that compromise meant doing things for the other person. So she ended up giving Mark the larger closet, the best cabinet space in the bathroom, and the best drawers in the dresser. But not only did he not appreciate this, he also claimed all of the room under the bed for his exercise equipment, and a cabinet in the kitchen for his photography equipment. Lisa began to resent this, and finally discussed it with Mark. They rearranged all of their storage space so that it was fair for both of them, and Lisa said that they learned a lot about compromising and communication from the experience.

One way to solve some of the issues you will be dealing with when you first get married is to make a list of issues on which you can't agree. At some point, sit down to discuss these issues, and work out a fair way to solve each of them. For instance, let's say that you want the television in the living room, and he wants it in the bedroom. And you don't like to answer the phone during dinner and he does. Well, if the phone during dinner issue is more important to you than it is to him, have it your way during dinner, and let him keep the television in the bedroom. That way, both of you get your way on the issues that you feel strongest about, and there won't be any lingering resentment.

All Those "Things"

There is another issue that can be difficult to deal with when you first get married, and that is dealing with each other's "things." Naturally he wants to keep the black and orange four-foot trophy he won at the Halloween ball, and she wants to display her prize collection of antique hats. But what's going to make a place "the two of yours" is how you compromise on these things.

One man said that his new wife wanted him to get rid of all his "bachelor furniture." He was very attached to his recliner chair, and to several other pieces of furniture. He couldn't understand why she felt so strongly about throwing the furniture away. He had never seen her as a "nag" before, but this really bothered him.

He told me that they finally sat down and talked about it, and she said that it was not merely that she didn't like the furniture, she just felt that it represented his single, wild days, and it bothered her to be reminded that she wasn't always the only woman in his life. This he could understand. So to make her happy, he got rid of everything except for his recliner chair. This was a good compromise, and worked well for both of them.

It is important to remember that people become very possessive about items that they may have had for a good portion of their lives. The items have somehow become a part of them. To ask them to get rid of them just for aesthetic reasons might sound cruel. But if the sight of the item is going to cause you to lose weeks of sleep, you need to have a discussion about it. Of course you don't need to have this conversation the second you get married, but when the timing is right, sit down, and maybe even make another list so that each person gets to keep things that are most important to him or her, or each person has to get rid of things that are equally important to him or her. Compromising on these issues is a good way to learn to work out even more important issues that will arise in the future.

Dealing with Change

Often, when two people get married, and as they are becoming a team, each person starts to realize that the other person is changing. After two years of marriage, one partner cries out in anger, "You're not the person I married!" Of course not! And I should hope not! If a person hasn't grown and changed in two years, it's a pretty sad commentary on that person's state. To live is to change. We grow as individuals, we grow as a team, we grow as parents, we grow as professionals. What is important in a marriage is that you manage your growth to coincide with your mate's, and that you keep communicating your changes and growth, so that your mate can continue to "know" you.

Wendy told me that she never knew what real communication was until she had been married for three years. In the first three years of her marriage to Don, their communication consisted of sharing their daily experiences. Even when they got upset with each other, their communication just consisted of saying sorry and moving on.

Don and Wendy hadn't realized how much they had changed since they had gotten married. When they had first been married, he had wanted kids right away and she had been the one to put it off until she finished graduate school. In three years, he had advanced a great deal in his career, derived a great deal of satisfaction from it, and was offered a big promotion out of state. At the same time, she had built up a nice social life, was very active in community life, and was now ready to have children. Here they were, with two separate agendas.

It took many discussions, a lot of realigning their shared goals, and, of course, a lot of compromise. But they did manage to decide to decline the promotion and start a family. However, the biggest result that came out of these discussions was a better level of communication and a strong commitment from both of them to share their changes with each other.

Some changes we make are deliberate. An example might be working on ourselves so that we don't lose our tempers quite so often. Or trying to be more caring to our spouses. These types of changes can benefit greatly from supportive mates who give us constant encouragement and makes us proud of our efforts. Sometimes we make changes to better ourselves, and sometimes we make changes at the requests of our partner, like being on time more often. It is important that we give special acknowledgement to our mates for making these types of changes. These deliberate changes are very valuable in our lives and are very productive in good, solid relationships.

And then there are changes of which we may not be aware. Even our spouses may see things that we do not see. Maybe we are becoming too careless with our household chores. Or maybe we don't cherish our relationships as much as we used to. Or maybe we are more thoughtful than we used to be. These changes, both positive and negative, have some underlying causes. Often it is valuable to figure out what they are. In the case of not cherishing the relationship, maybe the underlying cause is that your spouse yells at you. By knowing this, you can take actions to correct the behavior. On the other hand, in the case of becoming more thoughtful, maybe the underlying cause is that you feel thoroughly taken care of by your mate. By knowing this, you can acknowledge your mate for the behavior, and let your mate know the positive effect of his or her actions.

Brian said that he had been very unhappy in his marriage. His wife Amy seemed to take him for granted, and they seemed to argue about petty things all the time. Finally he went to speak to an older friend of his who was one of his role models. Brian's friend told him to start treating Amy like solid gold: Bring her flowers, and act as if she were the most magnificent woman on the planet!

Brian told me that at the time he laughed at the advice, but he followed it anyway. The result was that Amy began to cherish him and to treat him like gold, too. Before, while he had been busy making his wife wrong for all her behaviors, the roots of her behavior were partly his responsibility, too. When he changed his actions, she changed hers.

There are also changes that come from external sources. Examples of these might be a career change, a move, having a child, loss of a loved one, or other major occurrences in your lives. What is most important in these types of situations is that the two of you work through the changes together. All too often, people go through major changes in a kind of daze, just getting done what needs to get done without really communicating to their spouses how they feel about these changes. A spouse is there for comfort and commiseration. Use this precious resource. Going through these changes alone can be very lonely, and can even put a strain on your relationship. It is so valuable to share these experiences with each other by talking about how you feel about them. Your relationship will really grow because of it, and the bond that the two of you have will get stronger and stronger.

When Paula's father died, all she wanted was to be left alone. She withdrew from everybody, and no matter how much her friends tried, she wouldn't let anyone reach out to her. I was so moved by how her husband was able to deal with this situation. He gave her the room to grieve on her own, but let her know that when she was ready, he was there for her. After two days, she finally let him share her pain. Now, after the crisis, I can clearly see a closeness that I had not seen before.

Creating Your Future
Being a team also means creating your future together. Many

people think about their futures. They daydream about what they'd like to do, where they'd like to go, and what they'd like to have. They may be working toward many of these things, but they overlook the most important asset they have going for them. They don't share these ideas with their spouses. Maybe they are embarrassed, maybe they don't want their spouses to expect too much from them, or maybe they know that it's different from what their spouses want. But if people could just get over their apprehension about this, and sit down to discuss it, the whole world would open up to them! Then every marriage could become a powerful team driving toward the same future together!

Scott never told his wife his dream that one day, when they were all settled and secure in their lifestyle, he would like to do a lot of charity work for the community. When he was asked to join the board of a local charitable organization, he couldn't decide if the timing was right or not. He still didn't feel financially secure enough to put his energy into non-income-producing areas.

He decided to consult his wife about it, and her enthusiasm was overwhelming. She said that he would never feel that the timing was right, and not only did she support him in the idea, she wanted to help him in any way she could. Now, several years later, they do a lot of charity work together, and not only has their relationship become stronger than ever, their social life has grown a lot as well.

The fact is that when you keep your goals private, they don't have much power. They can die on the vine while no one notices. When you share your goals with your spouse, they become real. They come to life. It is even better if you write them down together and make a plan on how to accomplish them. Working together to create your future is one of the most powerful and satisfying ways to really bond with someone and feel that the two of you are full partners in this game called life!

After the Honeymoon
The glow of the wedding will last a long time, and you will have memories to cherish forever. But soon the realities of daily life will be upon you, and a kind of disillusionment will set in. This is very normal. Especially if you had a very large wedding. Now there seems to be nothing big on the horizon, nothing to plan, and nothing urgent to do. It is kind of peaceful, but many people have a "what's next?" kind of feeling. The only thing that's next is being together. After a short time of feeling a bit lost and disoriented, most people fall right

into the wonderful routine of being married to the ones they love most in the world. Don't let this initial period worry you, or make you think that it's all been a terrible mistake. If it helps, pick a project to work on together—maybe fixing up the living room, or laying a new kitchen floor. This will help you to adjust to the idea that you are settling into a new life.

And, one important part of your marriage should be to do special things together. Go to the restaurant you went to on your first date. Visit the place where you got married. Go out for ice cream at midnight. Watch your favorite old movie and curl up together with some popcorn and cookies. Take each other out for no special occasion. And make all birthdays and holidays great festivities. Life seems to go so fast, and as the days melt into weeks, it is these special occasions that stand out in our mind many years later.

NOTEBOOK

1. How do you plan to organize the logistics of your wedding?

_____

_____

_____

_____

_____

_____

_____

2. What books do you plan to read?

_____

_____

_____

_____

_____

_____

_____

3. What issues are you sure will come up with the families regarding your wedding?

_____

_____

_____

_____

_____

_____

_____

4. How do you intend to handle them?

_____

_____

_____

_____

_____

_____

_____

5. What obstacles do you foresee in your wedding plans?

_____

_____

_____

_____

_____

_____

_____

6. How do you intend to overcome them?

_____

_____

_____

_____

_____

_____

_____

7. What problems do you foresee in your relationship with your mate during this time?

_____

_____

_____

_____

_____

_____

_____

8. How do you intend to handle them?

_____

_____

_____

_____

_____

_____

_____

9. What issues do you foresee will get in the way of your staying committed?

_____

_____

_____

_____

_____

_____

_____

10. What issues do you foresee in your mate's way of staying committed?

_____

_____

_____

_____

_____

_____

_____

11. What talks do you need to have with your mate to handle these issues?

_____

_____

_____

_____

_____

_____

_____

12. Are the issues between the two of you becoming big enough that you need outside help? If so, where do you intend to go?

_____

_____

_____

_____

_____

_____

_____

13. If you are feeling the "bail syndrome," who do you intend to talk to in order to work it out?

_____

_____

_____

_____

_____

_____

14. Who do you anticipate will not be supportive of your marriage or wedding plans?

_____

_____

_____

_____

_____

_____

15. How do you intend to deal with this?

_____

_____

_____

_____

_____

_____

16. What will it take for you to give up your "me" mentality and switch to a "we" mentality?

_____

_____

_____

_____

_____

_____

17. What resistance do you have to becoming a team?

_____

_____

_____

_____

_____

_____

18. Make a list of ways of doing things that your partner does differently from you:

Your way: Partner's way:

_____   _____

_____   _____

_____   _____

_____   _____

_____   _____

_____   _____

_____   _____

19. Go through the list in question 18 and each take a turn choosing who gets his or her way on each specific item.

20. Make a list of "things" that you are each attached to, that you each dislike:

Your things: Partner's things:

_____   _____

_____   _____

_____   _____

_____   _____

_____   _____

_____   _____

_____   _____

_____   _____

_____   _____

_____   _____

21. Go through the list in question 20 and each take a turn choosing things to get rid of or to keep.

22. What is your natural reaction to change?

_____

_____

_____

_____

_____

_____

_____

_____

_____

23. What deliberate changes are you in the process of making now?

_____

_____

_____

_____

_____

_____

_____

_____

24. What deliberate changes is your mate in the process of making?

_____

_____

_____

_____

_____

_____

_____

25. What external changes are you going through with your partner, and what are you doing to deal with these changes? (For example, career changes, moves, loss of loved one.)

_____

_____

_____

_____

_____

_____

_____

26. Write down your daydreams about the future:

_____

_____

_____

_____

_____

_____

_____

_____

_____

_____

_____

_____

_____

_____

_____

_____

_____

_____

_____

_____

_____

_____

_____

_____

_____

27. Discuss these with your partner. Write down your partner's daydreams about the future:

_____

_____

_____

_____

_____

_____

_____

_____

_____

_____

_____

_____

_____

_____

_____

_____

_____

_____

_____

_____

_____

_____

_____

_____

28. Make out a simple or complex plan on how you intend to work toward or accomplish these daydreams:

_____

_____

_____

_____

_____

_____

_____

_____

_____

_____

_____

_____

_____

_____

29. After the honeymoon, what fun project can the two of you work on together to make your place "yours"?

_____

_____

_____

_____

_____

_____

30. Make a long list of "special" things you can do together for future reference!

_____

_____

_____

_____

_____

_____

_____

_____

_____

_____

_____

_____

_____

_____

_____

_____

_____

_____

_____

_____

_____

_____

_____

_____

Conclusion

BY NOW, YOU have done a lot of work toward finding and marrying the right mate for you. You have learned what you should look for, and how you will know when you've found it. You have learned about the emotional and environmental obstacles that stand in your way. You have learned the best places to find your mate and how to prepare for marriage. You have learned how to manage this project, and how to keep yourself motivated. And you have learned how to develop a stable relationship so that your marriage will last a lifetime.

If you aren't already engaged or married, you are probably closer now than you have ever been. You probably also have a clearer idea of what you are looking for than ever before. The key now is persistence. As we discussed in the very beginning, this is not an easy project. It takes time, and it can often be discouraging. But at least now you have a clear road to walk down, rather than aimlessly wishing and hoping that your life will work out. Now you have all the tools that you need to *make* it work out.

And it does take a while to get used to this new approach. For instance, Sandra felt that using the index cards on a first date was contrived. But as she continued using them over time, she was able to garner all of the necessary information in a very natural and pleasant way. In my own search, I didn't start out telling perfect strangers that I was getting married that summer. But after months of hard work, it became easier to network and to overcome my own feelings of awkwardness. If I had given up one stranger too soon, I never would have met my husband. You always need to think that your mate is just behind that next unturned stone! There are always difficulties when trying something new. What will make the difference to your success is sticking to your plan, even when you don't have any positive results yet. I know it's hard, but it usually is when the payoff is so big.

If you are having difficulty progressing in a particular area, try to figure out why. It might be helpful to reread the chapter on that subject, or do the notebook section of that chapter over again. Sometimes there are subconscious reasons why we just can't seem to move forward. Talking to someone may help; focusing your attention on another area of your plan may give you time to think clearly about the subject. I know that I have a tendency to avoid areas that are difficult, but when it came to getting married, I was more motivated than usual to overcome the obstacles in my way. I hope that I have given you enough assistance in identifying your own obstacles that you have gained the ability to push yourself forward on this project. Keep remembering that all you need to do is to find *one* person!

I would love to hear your comments and success stories! There is a marriage follow-up form at the end of this book; I hope you will be filling it out soon. Again, I wish you a life filled with joy and happiness. May you share it with someone very special!

Index

Get Married Now

Marriage Follow-up Form
(photocopy this form to fill out)

Today's Date: _____

Name: _____
(Your name will be strictly confidential)
Address: _____

City/Zip: _____

Age: _____ Male/Female: _____

Occupation: _____ Phone: _____

1. What date did you get engaged: _____

2. What date are you / did you get married: _____

3. How did the book assist you in finding your mate?

_____

_____

_____

4. What obstacles did you have to overcome to get married?

_____

_____

_____

5. Additional comments: _____

_____

_____

Mail this form to: Get Married Now, *Bob Adams, Inc., 260 Center Street,*
Holbrook, MA 02343.
Responses become the sole property of Bob Adams, Inc.
Sorry, but responses cannot be returned.

About the Author

Hilary Rich has been coaching people on how to get married for three years, using the plan that she created to find and marry her own husband. She currently teaches the popular Get Married Now seminar. She has worked as a business manager, a volunteer director, as a news reporter and radio announcer, and graduated *cum laude* and Dean's List from Boston University. Ms. Rich has served on the Board of Directors of the Los Angeles Mozart Orchestra and Jewish Family Services of Santa Monica. She lives with her husband Steven, a physician in West Los Angeles, and their baby daughter, Aliza.